A CHILD: YOUR CHOICE

Jean Shapiro

Over the past nineteen years, Jean Shapiro has been *Good Housekeeping* magazine's 'agony aunt', answering readers' letters on myriad problems and dilemmas. She was also, for fifteen years, Editor of the family section of *Good Housekeeping*. Jean Shapiro is author of the *Good Housekeeping Baby Book* (1977), the *Baby and Child Record Book* (1981), and *On Your Own: A Practical Guide to Independent Living* (Pandora, 1985). She is married, with children and grandchildren, and lives and works in London.

PANDORA PRESS HANDBOOK

A CHILD: YOUR CHOICE

Jean Shapiro

*A candid, everyday account
of the pleasures and pitfalls of
motherhood*

New York and London

First published in 1987 by Pandora Press
(Routledge & Kegan Paul Ltd)
11 New Fetter Lane, London EC4P 4EE

Published in the USA by
Routledge & Kegan Paul Inc.
in association with Methuen Inc.
29 West 35th Street, New York, NY 10001

Set in Palatino in 9 on 11 point
by Pentacor Ltd., High Wycombe, Bucks
and printed in the British Isles
by The Guernsey Press Co Ltd
Guernsey, Channel Islands

Library of Congress Cataloging in Publication Data

Shapiro, Jean, 1916–
  A child.

  (Pandora handbook)
  Bibliography: p.
  Includes index.
  1. Motherhood. 2. Choice (Psychology) I. Title.
HQ759.S46155 1987 306.8'743   87–9878

British Library CIP Data also available
ISBN 0–86358–073–4 (c)
ISBN 0–86358–195–1 (p)

CONTENTS

ACKNOWLEDGMENTS

My thanks are due, firstly, to the many women whose views and experiences are quoted in this book, and secondly to the Women's Reproductive Rights Information Centre which put me in touch with numbers of them. The readers of *Good Housekeeping* who reacted to my articles on motherhood helped me, too. Finally I want to thank Rose Shapiro for the many unplanned discussions we have had which have helped me to clarify some of the ideas here expressed. To all these people I am very grateful.

INTRODUCTION

One of the regularly-recurring questions to agony aunts is 'ought I to have a baby?' The writer is under pressure from custom or the needs of her husband or relatives; or she's unsure about her relationship with her partner; or she's concerned (too concerned? she asks) about the demands of her career. Perhaps she likes children but can't stand babies; or she may be terrified of childbirth; or afraid of becoming a cabbage. Is she too young? Or now she's in her late thirties, would pregnancy be too risky?

It was because I was on the receiving end of questions like these, and especially because, as a mother and grandmother, I was worried by the perennial media hype on the unalloyed joys of parenthood, that from the early 1970s onwards I wrote a number of articles on the choice that women have to opt out of motherhood, if that's what they want. I tried, too, to examine the reality behind the romantic pictures presented to young women – the hard work, the long-term responsibility, the sleepless nights, the radical changes in life-style that having a baby so often entails.

Many readers responded with relief that a women's magazine was at last saying these things. Others admitted that being a mother wasn't always what it was cracked up to be – but that in their experience it had proved ultimately rewarding and something they would never have missed out on. Some were bitter about the toll that being a mother had taken on them – the lack of respect from husbands and children for all the sacrifices they had made in bringing up a family. And of course others saw motherhood as women's ultimate destiny, and totally rejected the idea that they have any other means of fulfilment.

All of these views find expression in this book. I wrote it because I believe that it's only by exploring them, and listening to other women's experiences, that the individual can find a basis for her own, rational decision in this very personal and individual matter.

So anyone expecting to be told 'yes, go ahead', or 'no, you're better off without children' won't find these answers here. What I hope she *will* find is a wide-ranging discussion of the pros and cons and a glimpse of what being a mother – or deciding not to have a baby – might mean to her.

Since those articles were written in the 1970s and early 1980s more options have opened up. More women are waiting until their mid- or late thirties before embarking on pregnancy; single women are deciding to go it alone rather than form a relationship with an unsatisfactory partner solely in order to provide a child with a living-in father; lesbian couples are having children by the various means available to them. But while women truly have more choices, the right choice is not necessarily easier to arrive at. This book might help.

Jean Shapiro

Since many of the people quoted in this book wished to remain anonymous, I have substituted pseudonyms wherever first names only appear. When both first and surname are used the names are the actual ones of the women quoted.

PART ONE

CHAPTER 1

A QUESTION OF IMPORTANCE
THE BIGGEST DECISION OF YOUR LIFE?

What's the biggest decision you'll ever have to make?
Deciding whether or not to stay on at school after
sixteen; what job or career to aim for; when to leave
home; where to live; whom to live with; even
whether or not to marry – and to whom. These are all
very important decisions, and they can have far-
reaching effects. But in general they affect only you or
perhaps one other adult. And in most cases, if you
find you've made a mistake, you can change your
mind without a great deal of harm done.

Having a baby is different. Any decision you make
is certainly going to affect your future life and
probably that of your partner or friend. But more
importantly, if you decide to have a child you're
effectively creating another human being, and that
human being is going to be your responsibility – a
shared one, perhaps, but nevertheless primarily her
parents' – for many years to come. Her health, her
welfare, and a great deal of what happens to her in
her life are going to be shaped by you. You can't
detach yourself from your *child* without the risk of
great damage to her and a sense of failure and guilt in
yourself.

In the face of such awesome responsibility it's not
surprising that a thoughtful woman will stop and
take stock. Of course it's only in the last few decades
that she's actually had the 'luxury' of doing this.
Some women are even somewhat envious of pre-

vious generations who didn't have to make this choice. When marriage was the goal – or fate – of every 'normal' woman, childbearing was the almost inevitable sequel. No one asked her whether she really wanted children, or whether she wanted just one or half a dozen. Having children was her job, providing sex and babies for her husband was what she had to do in return for the security and status that marriage offered her. To question that would have been to question everything about the society she lived in.

Now there is a choice, and there are many factors that have made this possible. The availability of contraception, of course, is the key; but contraceptive methods wouldn't have been developed as they have without other, radical changes. Better public health and medical advances have ensured that in the West, every baby born has a good chance of survival. We no longer have to have a large number of children to ensure that a few survive to help their parents in their old age.

Women have become more independent, as a result of better education and their increased economic clout; they don't have to depend on men for their very survival, and they don't have to depend on producing children for a sense of fulfilment and personal worth. They don't *have* to; and many women are leading freer lives as a result of these changes. But it would be unrealistic to deny that despite everything, many of the old pressures remain. Girls are still brought up to believe that 'settling down' accompanied by having babies, is the ideal they must aim for. It's very hard for someone to reject these ideas, which are so relentlessly beamed at her by parents, teachers, magazines and advertisers. And, however free of their influence we may believe ourselves to be, there aren't many of us totally unaffected by them. Life experience and our own intelligence may tell us that we're being brainwashed. Emotionally though, it may be a different story. Any women who has consciously and explicitly rejected the pressures knows how easy it is to be driven on to the defensive, how 'different' she's made to feel because she's chosen childlessness, a lesbian way of life or celibacy. Very often she can only feel comfortable in the company of others who have made similar choices.

It's only comparatively recently that the conspiracy to present only the positive side of motherhood has been partially broken. Being a parent can, of course, be a rewarding and exciting and deeply satisfying experience. But to present it as unalloyed joy isn't fair. Women who accept the propaganda and then find that somehow they fail to get the promised rewards often don't realise that it's not they who have failed, but the relatives and friends and media who have failed *them* by being less than realistic and truthful.

In the following chapters we'll look at the experiences of some women who feel they've been badly let down by the external pressures and the motherhood myths they've been fed since their own childhood. But there are many others who do know that being a mother isn't always a picnic, but still wonder whether they'd be missing out if they rejected the choice.

SELF-FULFILMENT?

And even if we *could* detach ourselves from the powerful pressures put upon us to procreate – by family, friends, the media, 'society' – are we actually able to detach ourselves from our own inner feelings which may be telling us that motherhood is part of a woman's self-fulfilment? Life goes in stages – perhaps it's 'natural' that an adult woman should want to set a seal on her adulthood by having a baby? Without having children, would she be stuck in a sort of permanent adolescence?

From this idea flows another. Should we break the human chain that has led to our birth and that of our parents and grandparents and their ancestors, way back into pre-history? We may feel that it's a bad time to be thinking of adding another link to that human chain – famine, disease and the possibility of the ultimate destruction of a nuclear war make it an uncomfortable time to be alive. But we're here; that unconceived baby is not. Do we inflict our ills upon another being, if it can be avoided? Or do we see this as defeatist? Can we and our offspring make the world a better one, so that the generations to come will thank us for the gift of life?

MIXED RACE

Couples coming from different ethnic backgrounds often worry about possible discrimination or racism directed against any children they might have. Would they or their child be strong enough to cope with this? Is it fair to inflict the problems they themselves have met on a vulnerable child? No one can lay down rules about this: we can judge only by our own experience, the kind of community we live in, the sort of support likely to be forthcoming from family, neighbours and friends. Someone who believes very passionately in the need to maintain her or his racial identity will react quite differently from someone who feels that the only hope of future harmony lies in integration. Most people know families where 'mixed race' children seem to have had very few problems at school or in the wider community; they also know others where such children have been the targets of teasing, bullying or worse.

'I either ignore them or tell them I'm proud to be half-and-half. It's much more interesting, I say, to have two sets of grandparents who're so different.' That's how one fourteen year-old has coped with playground name-calling which, she says, does really come from only a few, though noisy, 'thugs' at her comprehensive school. Another child who has coped with similar behaviour points out that most people get bullied or attacked sometimes – on grounds other than race. 'You have to be tough, and you have to have friends,' he says. 'And of course you are better off in a school where the teachers aren't racist. Ours aren't: the deputy head is black and we have some Asian teachers, too; the white ones also make an effort!'

These are some of the fundamental questions the individual has to ask herself – and which by her own decision and her own action she has to try to answer.

MANIPULATION?

A seventy year-old grandmother looks with some cynicism at the current rush into motherhood by middle-class feminists in their thirties, saying, 'I've seen it all before.' She goes on:

'Are they sure they're not being manipulated? If you look back over what's happened to women over this century, a pattern emerges. "Fashions" change – but they're more than fashions. They're responses to subtle political pressures which make people believe they're choosing what they want, when in fact they're just doing what the current climate seems to require, and dictate. Early in the century – up to the Second World War, in fact – "rational" and "scientific" motherhood was preached. You had to stay at home, of course, and be a *good* mother, and the good mother was someone who treated her baby like a machine, didn't allow "weak" feelings of "self-indulgence" to break the strict code of self-discipline that made you refuse to pick your baby up and cuddle her because this would lead to *spoiling*. Naturally the majority of mothers broke the rules – but how guilty they were made to feel when they did! Then, after the war, came the Spock generation. Once more, mother stayed at home and produced at least three children (under-population – of whites, of course – was the bogey). And this mother was a slave to her family. They needed freedom to express themselves; they mustn't be stunted in the development of their personalities or thwarted in their wishes by any claim by the slavemother that she might sometimes want satisfaction of *her* needs. Back to the home, out of the labour market and into consumerism – that's what I think it was all about.

Then as a reaction, along came the women's movement, telling women they had a right to develop *themselves*, to get education, compete for jobs. And the Pill made "family planning" more of a reality than it had ever been before. In the 'fifties and 'sixties, an expanding economy in the West needed women's labour and women's skills – just so long as the *working wife's* activities didn't interfere too drastically with family life. Once more we had droves of guilty women – those who were guilty about "neglecting" their children and those who were ashamed of being "just a housewife."

Well, of course, that couldn't last. From about 1970 onwards there were rumblings of reaction, faint at first. Women's magazines began to question whether the working wife was really fulfilling herself, whether she was trying too hard to be like a man. With the rise in unemployment, accelerated since 1979, women in work outside the home began to feel (yet again) guilty about taking jobs they didn't *need*; and government cuts meant that the long-promised nurseries and nursery schools weren't forthcoming. Child-minding problems forced many women back into the home, soon to be joined by others who had been made redundant. As a partial solution to the problems – and to help with the family income when a male partner, too, became unemployed – there has been an increase in part-time work for women. It's low-paid, low-status, and insecure; even worse is the homework which many mothers are forced to take as their contribution to the household.

I think that all this provides fertile ground for politicians and others to extol the virtues of Victorian values – back to the home again, you women! And while you're about it, forget all those silly ideas about ways of fulfilling yourselves that don't include motherhood! Work part-time, if you must, but it wouldn't be good for you to make things too easy. And if you're doubtful, we can find all sorts of reasons, in history, sociology, biology and psychology, why being a mother is your finest achievement as a woman.

'So it's "science" once more to the rescue of patriarchy.'

This is a simplistic view of the current urge to reproduce that seems to be affecting women who grew up during the feminist upsurge of the 1970s. But it seems worthy of consideration by anyone who thinks that she just might be following lemming-like in the wake of a movement of thirty year-old plus feminists towards pregnancy. It's often very difficult to distinguish genuine feelings from mere trends and fashions, to know when you're being manipulated and when you have a real, informed choice. But in a matter as important as choosing or rejecting motherhood, it's as well to be aware of the pressures put upon you by your peers, and by the forces that have, in turn, affected them. Who can say that she's *un*affected by current ideas?

Trend, fashion or whatever – the possibility that we're in for another baby boom is borne out by the figures for 1985, which show that the birth rate in England and Wales rose by more than 3 per cent. Moreover, the fastest-growing group of mothers is the one comprising women of 30 to 34. Out of every 1,000 women in this age group, 77 had babies in 1985 – a contrast with 1977 when the rate was 59 per 1,000. However, only 24 women per 1,000 over 35 had babies. Over 40, only 5 per thousand.

'ACCIDENTAL' PREGNANCY

A particularly difficult situation is faced by someone who hasn't quite made up her mind about a future pregnancy, and then suddenly finds that she is, in fact, pregnant. Was it contraceptive failure, an 'accident', carelessness, or did she, consciously or unconsciously, take a risk? And in any case, what now is to be done about it?

There are plenty of people around who will moralise about the fecklessness of the girl or woman who becomes 'accidentally' pregnant. These 'risk-takers', they say, all had every opportunity to learn about contraception and unless they're very young (in which case recent court rulings and pronouncements from authority have made them scared about the possible consequences of getting contraceptive advice as their confidences might be breached) doctors and clinics are available in every locality. Why didn't they use them?

The answer in most cases is that in fact, they did. A majority of married women and those in stable hetero-sexual relationships have used contraception, according to the research. Contraceptive failure *is* a possibility, though in the case of the Pill, doctors tend to prefer to call it 'user failure'. Isobel Allen's study, published in 1985, however, reveals that 28 per cent of interviewed women with unwanted pregnancies have used contraception in the past but become pregnant when they either cease to do so regularly, or didn't take precautions on one particular occasion. Some of these women explain that they believed that they weren't, or were no longer, fertile. They had had unprotected intercourse sometimes over months or years, without becoming pregnant. Or they became pregnant following a change of partner: because they had not conceived with a former partner, they had assumed that they themselves were infertile, when in fact it was the former partner whose sperm production was abnormal.

But the research reveals something else. There are women whose motives for 'allowing' themselves to become pregnant may be obscure, even to themselves. Some admit that they may have 'taken risks' in order to test their marriage or relationship. Things were going badly, but maybe a pregnancy would bring the partners together again; or by getting pregnant the woman would find out whether or not her partner was responsible enough to father a child (if he pressed for an abortion, perhaps that would prove that he wasn't the right kind of man and she could break off the relationship and try again).

On page 21 we look at the very intense feelings that many women have about their *wholeness* as women. It's not only the continuity of human life on earth that dictates these strong feelings, but their belief that reproduction is tied up with the self and their conception of themselves. Childbearing is an experience that is vital to this sense of self. But what if – for some reason – a woman who believes this can't, in fact, produce a child: after all figures show that at least 10 per cent of women can't? It's this feeling that is probably behind the so-called risk-taking that causes some women to become 'accidentally' pregnant. They're testing out not a relationship, but *themselves*. Getting pregnant, however inconvenient the timing, answers the questions in the only possible way. Yes, they can – because they have.

What they, and the other 'risk-takers' and victims of contraceptive failure now do about it will depend not only on their attitudes to abortion but also on their ultimate intentions. If, like one woman, you planned to have a baby in a year or two when you and your partner were settled in a house and he had completed his higher degree, you would probably not consider an abortion but suffer some discomfort in unsuitable accommodation, and some shortage of money. You would have advanced your ultimate plans by a couple of years. If like many others, you found that your partner walked out on you once he knew you were pregnant, or the pregnancy was the result of unpremeditated sex with someone you scarcely knew and certainly couldn't envisage as the father of your child, your decision would probably be very different.

Perhaps it isn't surprising that someone who has become pregnant largely because of a subconscious wish to test out her ability to conceive may, in the event, draw back from motherhood. A journalist in her late twenties confesses:

'I really don't understand myself, I normally behave like a rational person. Yet I knew what I was doing when my ex-boyfriend and I had sex without using contraceptives right at the most fertile time of my cycle. Did I want a baby? No, of course not. It was against common sense to think I could cope alone, with no partner and no money except what I can earn in my very full-time and demanding job. Yet honesty makes me admit that it wasn't an accident. So what was I trying to prove? I suppose it was my own fertility. But as a result I've had to go through an abortion – a difficult and emotionally painful experience. It's going to take me a while to get back my confidence in myself.'

This woman does want children and it was difficult for her to decide on an abortion. At considerable cost she now knows that pregnancy is a physical possibility. But, she says, she will never again run the risk of pregnancy until she's sure that she can provide a secure environment for a child.

Another woman, a secretary in her late thirties, says that she believes that when she 'forgot' to take the Pill on holiday with her it meant something:

'When I first knew I was pregnant, my reaction was that I'd been an absolute fool and that the only answer was an abortion. . . . But there were the usual delays, and by the time the whole thing had been fixed, I'd begun to feel that this was my baby, my last chance, probably, to have one. I talked it over with my boyfriend, and we decided against the abortion. He's married, and I think this situation has finally forced him to make up his mind to agree to a divorce. I'm still not sure whether it will work out between him and me, but I do trust him to take some responsibility for me and the baby. Some people will say that I've deliberately engineered this whole thing. I just don't know. All I do know is that I'm going to have a baby and I'm glad about it.'

Worry about ability to conceive would be resolved, of course, if, once a woman had made up her mind that she does want children, she just went ahead and tried. The advice of Barbara Jane, a member of an infertility self-help group described later in this book, is 'don't wait.' Barbara believes that this way no time is lost should it be discovered that there is some fertility problem, and she's quite convinced that once a positive decision is made obstacles can be swept aside; a good job, satisfactory housing – things like this can be goals too far ahead, and possibly unattainable.

PARTNERSHIP AT RISK?

Alison has lived with her boyfriend for nearly seven years. They plan to marry. She says:

'My main worries about pregnancy are to do with my freedom in the future and how it will alter my life and my partner's life. I know the sacrifices to be made and worry about how I will actually cope when the time comes. My partner and I have a great relationship and share household tasks etc. Ideally we would like to be able to job-share when we have children, so that we both have a chance to work in the outside world – *but* this isn't an ideal world and as I am now twenty-nine we feel we don't want to wait too much longer before starting a family. I worry about how we will be able to work things out and I hope that having a child doesn't upset our relationship.

'I think I've always thought I'd like children, but it has always been something for the future. I suppose my partner and I have been talking and thinking about it together, off and on, for the past two or three years: trying to decide whether or not to start a family. Basically we both wanted to – at the same time – but have also been considering the alternative (remaining childless) as an option.

'As I've said, I'd like to return to work. . . . When the time came, though, I might feel I don't want to. . . . In our present situation it would seem more sensible for me to work full-time and my partner to stay at home with the baby. He'd be prepared to do this. . . . I think I'd be jealous if he was at home with the baby all day – though I hate to admit it.'

Alison says that she's fully aware of the difficulties of parenthood – perhaps too aware. She believes that she really is prepared, in theory, but when the time comes she may get a shock:

'I've noticed that the older my friends are when they have their first child, the more prepared they are to talk about the difficulties – but I don't know if this is because the younger you are, the less "thinking" you do and the more you just get down to it and cope.'

POSTPONING THE DECISION

'I face a real dilemma' says one thirty year-old:

'I've never been totally convinced that I wanted to be a mother. Up until now, it's always been something I've felt I could leave until later on – the decision, I mean. Now I'm getting pressurised, partly because of my age, and partly because so many people tell me that I'm being selfish thinking of my own career rather than adding to the human race! Is there something in that, I wonder? My husband doesn't help – he sees the decision as something for me, which is fair enough, since I know I'd be the one to stay at home and look after the baby. But it does make things difficult.'

Another woman in her thirties also feels a sense of pressure. She isn't married and has a number of rather unsatisfactory relationships behind her. She knows that she wants children, but she's convinced that she shouldn't have a baby unless there's a good chance that the child will have a father around. She says:

'Several friends of mine are single parents. I see their struggles to manage alone, and I wouldn't want to be in that position. It seems to be pretty difficult when the child is a baby, but I think I could manage that. It's when problems crop up in the way the child is developing, or there's trouble with other children or at school that I think it's so hard for one adult to take the brunt of it all. Children seem to need two adults close to them, anyway, and it does seem that they're happier when those two adults are their actual parents.

'But, though I believe all that, I do so desperately want children that I can't wait much longer, and if no man comes along that I think I could share the next part of my life with and that I'd want to be the father of my child, I shall have a baby anyway – if I can. I hate the position I've got myself into – sizing up every man I meet to see if he fits the bill. It's like a woman's magazine story heroine waiting for "Mr Right" – and no doubt very off-putting to any sensible man.'

A third woman is equally convinced that she wouldn't want, and couldn't manage, to have a child on her own:

'Sure, I'd like to have a baby, but I definitely wouldn't even think of it unless I had a good and apparently permanent relationship. I don't know anyone I'd want to live with – so I may well land up childless. It's a sort of sacrifice and maybe a bleak prospect, but I think the alternative would be worse, for the child as well as for me.'

A number of the women whose stories are outlined in Jean Renvoize's book *Going Solo: Single Mothers by Choice* (1985) – all of whom opted for having a baby without a permanent male partner – did find the going very tough. Those who were lesbians, where the decision to have a baby had been made jointly with their partner, had experienced no more problems than the average heterosexual couple – within the family, that is. As we shall see later in this book, such difficulties as there were came from outside.

A QUESTION OF TIMING

All of these women feel that some pressure is on them to make up their minds when they are in their thirties. For many years now we've been told that the best and healthiest time to have a first baby is in the early twenties. This may still be true. For one thing, fertility does very slightly decline in the following years, so conception may be a little more difficult. And in the early twenties energy is usually high and a young woman may be better equipped to withstand the rigours of broken nights and breast-feeding after a possibly exhausting birth. But this is to look only at the physical aspect of childbirth. *Emotional* readiness may be something different.

In recent years there has been a tendency for the average age of women having their first child to go up – in 1985, 27 in England and Wales, compared with 26.2 in 1970. At the same time, because of better general health in the population, and advances in medical care in pregnancy and childbirth, the chances of successful pregnancy in an 'elderly' (that is over twenty eight) first-time mother have greatly increased. Even though fertility does decline after the twenties, it happens slowly, and now very many women can defer their pregnancy to their thirties – something that would have actually been quite risky to mother and child twenty years ago.

It's this possibility that has enabled many women to wait until they're past their twenties before making a decision – as the women quoted later have done. Some will have deliberately waited to 'sort themselves out' before having a baby. Those with careers to establish, giving them a solid work background when they return to their jobs after having children, feel they'll be at a great advantage. Increased confidence and self-understanding that the years have brought are other factors that make many women glad they waited. 'Looking back on what I was like in my early twenties makes me shudder to think how I could possibly have coped with being a mother,' says one thirty three year-old. And most important of all, by the time they're in their late twenties or early thirties most women have had sufficient experience to know whether the relationships they've formed are likely to be stable ones, or at least sufficiently stable to see them and their children through the first, taxing years.

But the years do pass – and what happens when you reach the crucial thirties, you want a child and, like some of the women quoted, you still haven't been able to feel confident enough about your personal relations to go ahead? Everyone knows the statistics about marriage breakdown – that one in three couples will be divorced. There's no way of knowing what happens to unmarried 'permanent relationships.' The likelihood is that these will eventually prove at least as unstable as more formal ones. What you may have to consider now is your ability to take the major share of responsibility for a child, if a break does occur; or how you would feel about handing such responsibility over to your partner; or what the chance of genuine, shared care would be; or whether you could envisage staying together for the sake of the child, despite incompatibilities or 'unfaithfulness'; or whether you already have, or are likely to have, solid support from friends and family to enable you to manage your life and your child's without the enormous problems that going-it-alone can involve. These considerations apply both to married and unmarried partnerships.

In later chapters we look at the options in more detail. The fact that the problem and the decision is a real one for you, because you really want a child, and time may be running out, is crucial and can be painful. If you're younger and healthy and can afford to wait before making a decision, perhaps you'd be wise to do so. But whatever your age and whatever your personal situation, looking at the facts, insofar as they're available, and at the experiences of other women, may help. That's what we aim to do in the following chapters.

NUCLEAR FEARS

Gill and Roger are a married couple who have firmly decided not to have children. They are deeply concerned about the state of the world today and very worried about the future. They see it as irresponsible to bring a child into such a world. 'Self-indulgent' they believe. 'I couldn't justify putting an innocent child at risk of nuclear war or some other form of slow annihilation' Gill says. 'OK – that may sound negative. Other people's consciences may tell them something different. But we're not going to be pressurised to have children, feeling as we do. We have to take responsibility for ourselves; that's quite enough.'

Another couple, while sympathising with this view, believe that it's no use struggling for a peaceful world if there are no children around to enjoy it. It's a token of faith in the possibility of change, they say, to have the children they want.

As an organisation for people who have firmly decided that they don't want children, BON (British Organisation of Non-Parents) publishes a number of leaflets for enquirers. As Debra Ziegler, Co-ordinating Chairman of BON says, it is 'a very small support and information organisation only, as we are not large enough any more to do a great deal of campaigning, since most of our members are professionals who have heavy time commitments elsewhere. However, we do answer a lot of post from people writing in for information on the choice to be childless.'

BON's literature expresses many of the ideas and asks many of the questions considered in this book, making a big point that '"responsible parenthood" should be based on an informed decision whether or not to have children', and stresses that through its publicity it gives you 'the opportunity to know that you are not unique or "freakish" and a chance to hear from or speak to others who feel the same way.' The question, says BON, should not be '"Why don't I . . . ? but why *do* I want a child?" Surely one should have good reason for doing something as irrevocable and important as creating another human being.'

SOBER ASSESSMENT

One of the situations discussed so far – or something very like it – applies to you. Each presents some difficulties and some challenges. But once you've faced them you're in a far better position to assess your needs and your probable future. You may have individual worries – we'll look at these in the next chapter – but you'll be a little clearer about general questions. And this means that you'll be in a better position to resist pressures to have, or not to have, your baby.

It's unlikely, though, that just reading a couple of chapters in this book is going to tip the balance. Unless you were already almost certain about trying now to get pregnant, you'll still have some doubts about the timing and possibly about having a baby at all. By all means listen to the advice and experience of your relatives and friends – they may have something valuable to offer. But in the long run it can be very unwise to succumb to the pressure from your parents – open or unspoken – to give them the grandchildren they seem to long for. The frustration experienced by many older women in the past has led them to see their value in life as simply their ability to care for children. When you and your sisters or brothers left home there may have been a void in your mother's life. Unconfident and untrained for anything but domestic activities, she hasn't any outside interests. A grandchild would give her back part of her role – the best part – and it's possible that this is the reason why she's pressing you to produce a baby.

Meeting her needs, though, isn't a good enough reason for you to change *your* life. You may feel you're being selfish and unkind in denying her her wish – after all, she might have had a pretty rotten deal out of life – but unless you're as certain as can be that it's your wish too, you'll have to resist. Maybe not for good; you may change your mind, or plan to have a baby in a few years' time. But it has to be understood that you're an independent person, you make your own decisions. Yielding to pressure now can lead to major problems – not least the possibility that, because you've done what your mother wanted on this occasion, you'll be expected to do what she says about managing the baby in the future. Conflicts between mothers and daughters can continue unresolved for years; they can be damaging to everyone and sometimes can be settled only by total withdrawal – a sad situation. You may understand your mother's needs, sympathise with them, but you don't have to accede to her demands.

Less easy to identify, because it's much more subtle, is a sort of 'spirit of the times', and the pressure to conform to it. This may appear in the guise of the seductive advertisements and articles in the women's magazines, the books and propaganda about the joys of childbirth. It may arise because of the dissatisfaction you may feel about your work and job prospects, or unemployment. If you're not going to be a successful worker, what about becoming a successful mother? There may be a competitive spirit between your partner and yourself. He's so successful, so good at everything that you think you're not good at – so what about opting out altogether from that kind of rat race?

And there's another kind of pressure that's experienced right now by many feminists who, in their youth in the 1970s were so busy, so involved in the women's movement, so sure that a future without encumbrances was right for them that they rejected the idea of becoming mothers. In their thirties now, they're having second thoughts. Have they been suppressing the biological urge to reproduce that they now feel so strongly? Are there satisfactions to be gained through motherhood that are just not offered by life without children? Are they missing out on an experience that is shared by the vast majority of women? These are the questions such women are now asking, and many of them are answering these questions in the affirmative. They're affirming their right to choose to be mothers and, for a time at least, to see this as central to their lives. Despite some unexpected health problems, pregnancy to such women is a time of almost ecstatic happiness. They may have morning sickness and feel exhausted at times, but they love to feel the baby's kicks, they feel good about their swollen bellies; they've made a decision and they accept it totally. Other women, seeing this, are bound to ask themselves the same questions – and perhaps come up with the same answers.

We've discussed in this chapter some of the options that may be open to you and some of the pressures you may be experiencing. Later in the book the views of individual women will be quoted – some of them women with the sort of questions and problems you may be having. Along with all the other influences surrounding you, their opinions, doubts and worries may help you to make up your own mind. Because that's what it's all about – you want to make an informed choice.

We'll look throughout this book at some of the problems that cause some women to think very long and hard about having a baby, and others to think in the light of experience that they might have arranged things differently.

WHY THE DOUBTS?

It may be helpful now to look at some of the reasons why a woman of any age may be troubled about the decision she feels she needs to take now or in the fairly near future.

You may be doubtful about having a baby because:

- You know that some babies are very demanding and you might find the stress and exhaustion of the first few months just too much.

- You know nothing about babies and you might do everything wrong.
- You might be the sort of person who would suffer from post-natal depression.
- You're scared of the pain and distress of the actual birth.
- You may not be the 'ideal' mother.
- You may find that you just don't like your baby, and you can't 'bond' with her.
- You can't imagine yourself as a full-time mother.
- You suspect your motives for having a baby; perhaps you're just dissatisfied with life as it is.
- Your child would be brought up without a father.
- Your child *might* be brought up without a father or a second parent-figure.

If these are your worries, we'll try to take a look at them in the following pages. Perhaps they do raise good reasons why you should avoid, or maybe postpone, pregnancy. Or perhaps they're just things you could think about and bear in mind if you do decide to go ahead. After all, the decision you make will be reached after a lot of weighing-up of pros and cons. That's why you're reading this book.

But no book, no counsellor, no doctor can tell you what is right for you. No one can guarantee that having or not having a baby won't turn out to be an enormous joy or a terrible mistake – or something in between. Only by looking at other women's lives and at the social, medical and personal-political facts can we hope to make a reasonably well-informed decision. Later in the book we'll try to look at the ways in which different life-styles and different sexual orientations may affect this decision. Married or single, with or without a long-standing heterosexual relationship, lesbian, celibate, living alone or as part of a collective, you're on the brink of making the choice between motherhood and childlessness. Perhaps in the following chapters you'll find help.

CHAPTER 2

NEGATIVE FEEDBACK
ARE SOME OF YOUR WORRIES JUSTIFIED?

If you're seriously considering getting pregnant, perhaps the greatest anxiety you have is the one that came top of the list on page 21 – would you really be able to cope?

First of all – do you really know what's involved? How much experience of real babies have you? You're probably wise enough to know that television advertisements and the charming pictures of happy mothers and lovely babies you see in baby books and magazines don't tell the whole story. Of course there will be off-days – and nights; but friends and neighbours seem able to cope, so why not you?

It's very possible that these friends and neighbours are as happy and fulfilled as they look, and that their babies eat, sleep and excrete to order and in conformity with the highest expectations of their parents and the baby books. But it's also possible that like most of us, these contented mothers are putting a good face on things, and that behind closed doors and drawn curtains there are times when exhaustion, desperation and feelings of overwhelming aggression towards their babies, their partners, the writers of baby books and a complacent society take hold.

'Why didn't anyone tell me?' is something that many mothers, and not only those of 'difficult' babies, cry to an indifferent world. It's true enough that everyone – from relatives, to the media, to advertisers – seems bound together in a conspiracy to tell us that, if only we manage things right, a new baby will be a joy that will quite outweigh any minor inconveniences we may suffer. But it's only fair to say that in recent years there have been quite a few publications, including some baby books, that have tried to stress that there may be problems, you may be overwhelmed and overtired in the first few weeks or months, and you may have to change quite radically your expectations of life-after-the-birth.

One health visitor who ran 'before' and 'after' classes for new parents was well used to the 'Why didn't anyone tell me?' plea. 'I did,' she reminded them, 'but you didn't want to know.' From experience she was well aware of the problems that might hit relatively unprepared parents, and without over-emphasising the difficulties they could face, she did try, before the birth, to discuss with the pregnant women and their partners the changes in life-style that a new baby would involve.

'They listened politely, but I don't think they really took anything in. At the first opportunity they changed the subject. If there was anything at the back of their minds about the future, it was a denial that these problems could really apply to them.'

It's possible, of course, to be over-pessimistic about your ability to cope. Discussions of 'baby blues' and post-natal depression can provoke anxiety, sometimes to such a degree that a woman may believe that some form of depression is almost inevitable. One mother reports that, so insistent were the staff in the maternity ward in asking her how she felt on the crucial days three to four that she became quite guilty when telling them that she was perfectly all right. She wondered whether the staff's obvious expectations of weepiness didn't sometimes act as a self-fulfilling prophecy.

BLUES OR DEPRESSION?

Nevertheless it is fair to report that, for whatever cause, social or hormonal, a large number of women do feel emotionally fragile, perhaps with a sense of guilty let-down, a few days after giving birth; but the good news is that this is usually a very temporary thing and not an experience that is ever likely to 'put off' a woman from having another baby. So it's hardly likely to dissuade the woman considering a first pregnancy from going ahead.

But perhaps your anxiety is about possible depression of a more long-term nature. You may have had depressive episodes in the past and wonder whether the stress of pregnancy and childbirth could bring about a recurrence. Or a close relative may have gone through a bad time after the birth of a child. In chapter 6 we'll be looking at some aspects of post-natal depression. Let's just note here that it's *not* inevitable that a history of clinical depression means that you'll be a candidate for post-natal depression. For one thing, your circumstances are probably now totally different from those that may have driven you into past despair.

FAMILIARITY BREEDS CONFIDENCE

If you are considering having a baby, it would be a good idea to try to get to know the babies of friends or relatives, and, of course, their older children too. You would be doing yourself, as well as their parents, a favour if you took over the care of a baby or toddler for a few hours when possible. Every ante-natal class includes several women who have never actually held a baby before, let alone fed one, soothed a distressed one, changed a nappy or wiped up messes. And if you haven't looked after a two year-old whose abounding energy involves her in behaviour that can threaten her life and limb and your sanity, you won't know how to channel it into safer and more constructive activities. Experience of babies and young children as they actually are may do more than anything else to help you make up your mind about having one of your own.

A 'GOOD ENOUGH' MOTHER

'I have absolutely no experience with babies,' says one woman, who does, she says, know all about older children, since she's taught the 'top' class in a primary school for several years.

'I think I'll be able to cope once the child reaches an age when it's possible to *reason* with it. But when you see babies and toddlers screaming their heads off and the mother looking at a total loss about what to do about it, I feel I am badly prepared. I'm sure I couldn't dish out the slaps and abuse that seem to be some people's way of shutting a child up, because that's not only against my principles but I don't think it works. How do you deal with a child who's too young to understand that it mustn't do dangerous things, grab other people's property and so on? I don't know. And I ask myself whether I'd be capable of devoting myself 100 per cent to thinking up ways of preventing these situations developing. What it amounts to is that I'm just too unsure of myself; I don't believe that being a good mother is something instinctive. If it were, you wouldn't see so many desperate women with unhappy, uncontrollable children around. If we could only give birth to five year-olds rather than babies I wouldn't be so ambivalent about getting pregnant!'

Susan is not worried about her ability to care for a baby:

'I think everyone considering pregnancy ought to try to think beyond the first few years. It must be very easy to be concerned, first, about your pregnancy and how you'll cope with that, and the birth. But I wonder how many people think ahead to what it will be like in twelve or fifteen years' time to be involved with a teenager. Looking back I realise what a dreadful time my parents must have had with me. My poor mother! Going through the menopause and having someone like me to cope with! I went completely wild, stayed out all night without telling my parents where I was, took off for days at a time, actually. Once or twice I was in trouble with the law. I bunked off school. I was rude – abusive. Of course they made their mistakes in handling me, but really I think they'd have had to be mixtures of saints and psychiatrists to be able to withstand the trouble I caused without putting a foot wrong sometimes.

'What have I learnt from all that? I suppose in theory I would try to be less confrontational and above all try to be less upset and anxious. But that's all very well in theory. I do know that when you're emotionally involved, as I suppose you inevitably are with your children, it must be very difficult to let things take their course, to be able to be confident that the girl will settle down in the end. I'm an emotional person. I really do worry about my ability to be sufficiently detached from the lives of any children I might have.'

There's another anxiety which is a very natural one, and which a majority manage to overcome – that's fear of childbirth itself. A woman who is really ashamed of her terror of the pain and the trauma says that she's constantly put off the idea of having children until some time in the indefinite future. She says it's made worse because:

'Other women go through it. They'll tell you how awful it was, but they seem to accept that just as part of the price you have to pay. I don't want to hear these horror stories, but in another way I do. They just confirm my feeling that I'm not the sort of person who can stand bad pain. After all, I suffer agonies *before* going to the dentist, worse, in fact than the pain he occasionally causes when I do go.'

Perhaps if she could accept that her fear is an exaggerated version of the apprehension that most women experience when thinking about their first childbirth, and treat it as such, finding out about relaxation techniques, pain relief and ways of overcoming what some might see as a phobia (which, like most phobias, usually has some 'real' basis), she will be able to go ahead and have the baby she and her husband want. There are organisations that could help, with information, reassurance and therapy – they're listed on pages 178–81.

What the examples of all these women illustrate are the very understandable reasons why it's possible to feel that you could fall short as a mother. What is lacking in them is the confidence – some people might call it over-confidence or complacency – that enables most women to go ahead with pregnancy, childbirth and bringing up children, in the belief that, on the whole, they'll be 'good enough' parents. Every one of us inevitably makes mistakes, but the results, on balance, are seldom as dire as we expect at the time. Before being paralysed with anxiety about real or imagined inadequacies, it's as well to understand that there are sources of help and advice if you're willing to seek them out, and that consistent back-up from partner, family, and good friends will help solve the majority of problems. Every aspect of life involves some sort of risk-taking and parenthood *can* be a high-risk area. But of course it needn't be: most adults seem to survive relatively unscathed from their upbringing. A majority of children thrive and appear to be happy. Why not you and yours?

A HARD LIFE?

Some years ago, researchers from the Thomas Coram foundation in London conducted interviews with over ninety couples in a London suburb at fixed intervals before and after the birth of a first baby. For 96 per cent of them, the main problem in the first six weeks of their baby's life was tiredness – hardly surprising, since on the night before the interview 75 per cent of the babies had woken at least once between midnight and six a.m. Many had also been 'unsettled', with long periods of wakefulness, during the previous day – 27 per cent having slept for only four hours or less. Even at the six-month interview, the proportion of parents who never felt tired had risen to only 7 per cent. Some of these mothers reported periods of intense or less intense depression, worry or psychological stress, though only three had sought medical treatment.

In chapter 5 we consider the sort of help that's available to parents having 'management' difficulties with their babies – the baby who cries excessively, the one who doesn't put on weight as she 'should', who doesn't sleep or who seems generally miserable. It's these problems that are common and worrying for a first-time mother. If she were able to appreciate before ever having the baby that they *are* common, that there *are* solutions to most of them, that help *is* available, and that in the vast majority of cases they lessen or disappear as the baby matures, she's better prepared if they do occur. It's a well-known fact that someone who's prepared for difficulties, or ordeals such as surgery, copes with stressful situations better when they arise. And there's always the chance that they won't!

We've already discussed some of the factors that may lead to unrealistic expectations of ourselves as women and mothers. What is the purpose of the glorification of motherhood, the idealisation of a woman as carer and nurturer? Are these ideas flattering and helpful, or do they really mask a perpetuation of women's role as mainstay of the home and family, the selfless provider of comfort for everyone but herself? 'Mothers' Day' is remembered once a year. Are a bunch of flowers and a cup of tea in bed one March Sunday the best she can hope for and be grateful for? And what if she has a strong suspicion that she doesn't really deserve even those minimal tokens of esteem? How do *you* feel: what sort of a mother would *you* be? You've got a lot of faults – you know about them, they've been pointed out to you often enough. No doubt about it, you're not perfect, and isn't it that sort of doubt about yourself and your capacities that is one of the things that makes you wonder about your ability to be a 'good mother'?

It's very hard for someone who has been brought up, as so many women have, in an atmosphere where unselfishness, deferring to others, never asserting herself or complaining of injustice are qualities to be admired and striven for, to accept that these 'ideals' might be questioned. Practically every baby book you're likely to read will quote the late Dr Winnicott's concept of the 'good enough' parent. But it's worth pointing out yet again that he didn't say 'perfect' or 'ideal', when describing what he felt to be adequate parenting. If you run your life reasonably efficiently, can feel close to others, with consideration for them as human beings but without undue deference; if you're averagely healthy and energetic and as secure as most in your relationships, who is to say you wouldn't be a 'good enough' mother? As we'll see in a later chapter, some women with quite severe disabilities – provided they have adequate back-up – can not only manage to experience successful and happy motherhood, but believe that their children are in no way disadvantaged.

THE 'UNLOVED' BABY

There's another doubt that clouds some women's thoughts when they are on the brink of pregnancy. Like most people, you often take instant likes and dislikes. How would it be if, unexpectedly, once you had your planned-for baby, you didn't like her or actually rejected her? Perhaps a difficult pregnancy or labour might affect your reactions to her; or you might have desperately wanted a boy and the baby was a girl (or vice versa); or the relationship with your partner, which you thought was a good one, had gone sour; or the much–wanted baby might have been found to be physically or mentally handicapped. All these – and more – are reasons why some women find that they can't love their babies as they 'should'.

Some of these reasons are linked with the depression mentioned earlier. They turn out to be non-existent, or much less serious, when the depression has lifted or its other causes removed. But if the dislike of or downright hostility to the child remains and is likely to cause emotional or physical damage, counselling or psychiatric help will be needed. Such situations, in the absence of other obvious factors in a woman's life, are rare; and again, the fear that such a problem might arise out of the blue is unlikely to be a reason why pregnancy should be avoided.

Much commoner is the experience of non-feeling towards the baby that may happen for a few days or weeks after her birth. This is worrying to someone who has believed that a mother instinctively loves her baby on sight. A 'cure' for this lack of maternal feeling is normally just the day-to-day physical care of the baby that most women feel bound to give. 'Go through the motions of affection,' says one woman doctor, 'and to your surprise one day you'll actually *feel* it.' This is advice to remember if you worry about your possible inability to 'bond' as everyone tells you you should.

MOTHERHOOD MYTHS

In fact the whole subject of 'bonding' has been called into question by psychology Professor Martin Herbert and social worker Alice Sluckin in their book *Maternal Bonding*. As they point out, all sorts of problems in children – failure to thrive, autism, and of course child abuse – have been blamed on lack of bonding with the mother. As the writers suggest, there may be many reasons why this 'all-important' bonding is impossible – the baby may be in a special care unit, for instance; and in some Asian cultures the process is actually discouraged: the mother handles the child as little as possible for several days after the birth. Does this foreshadow inevitable deprivation for the child in the future, as the experts would suggest would happen to a Western baby? And, as the researchers point out, attaching such importance to a process whose scientific validity they believe they've amply disproved is just another example of the way in which women can be brainwashed and blamed for being less than 'model' mothers, and the causes of all kinds of emotional problems in their children.

In the mid-1950s much was made by the 'experts' of the evidence produced by Dr John Bowlby and others that babies and children were adversely affected – indeed, marked for life – if for any reason their mother was absent. Although the research that led to this conclusion was carried out in institutions, where the children were indeed living in regimented inhumane conditions, deprived of affection, authority used this evidence to tell mothers that they ought to devote themselves 100 per cent to their babies. If they didn't, so the story went, their children would grow up unable to give or receive love, disturbed and unhappy. We can see how useful this theory was at a time when women were being discouraged from looking outwards from domesticity and finding fulfilment in roles other than motherhood.

Slowly this myth of 'maternal deprivation' which had such an influence on women for twenty or thirty years is giving way. We now realise that a child with a secure background is *not* going to be marked for life by his mother's temporary absence for social or work reasons. But another myth – the 'bonding' theory – has taken its place. It's important to question the thinking behind these theories which have had such a guilt-provoking effect on so many women. At the same time we can question our own belief that, because we can't envisage devoting our lives 100 per cent to the care of children, we may not be 'proper' mothers and therefore perhaps not fit to be mothers at all. If that's how you feel, it's worth remembering that many respect-worthy researchers have found that the children of working mothers or women who have absorbing outside interests are actually less prone to emotional or developmental problems than those of the full-time mother. This is not to say that you won't face criticism from many sources – especially if your child does present a problem of some kind – aimed at making you feel guilty of 'neglect'. Unfortunately the majority of working mothers, even if they're forced by necessity to work outside the home, have these guilt feelings. It's hard to resist this pressure – but when it happens remember that it's your life, and you have the right to run it as you like. It's only if you feel that work and a career are so all-absorbing for you that a baby could be an unwelcome diversion that you'd decide that motherhood was not for you. If, like most women, work is only part of your life, and relationships are equally or more important, you'll be able to face the undoubted difficulties of work-plus-family with confidence.

In chapter 8 we'll look at some ways of managing time off.

A SOFT OPTION?

When you are thinking of the timing of a career break, there's one possibility you should perhaps consider. Perhaps you feel dissatisfied with the way things are going at work. You may be in a boring or frustrating job. You may even be a bit jealous of your partner's relatively successful career, while *you* are in the doldrums, or fed up because your job is distasteful or not demanding or rewarding as you feel it should be for someone of your capabilities. It's not uncommon in such a situation for a woman to decide to drop out, get away from the rat race or a soul destroying routine: and to see having a baby as a soft option.

But soft option, as we have already noted, it very

seldom is. If you think that you may be allowing temporary setbacks at work to influence you unduly, should you perhaps hang on, meanwhile doing all you can to improve the position? Then, if eventually you decide that having your baby will fulfil a real need rather than making a choice dictated by boredom, difficulties with the boss or a sense of under-achievement, the decision is far more likely to lead to contentment.

BABY AS PEACEMAKER?

There used to be a belief that having a baby was a good way to patch up a fragile relationship. No agony aunt or marriage counsellor nowadays would suggest such a remedy. But that doesn't mean that no one in such a situation ever considers pregnancy as a way of hanging on. If things between you and your partner aren't going well, it's hardly likely that they'll improve under the strain of pregnancy and bringing up a child. At best, the result of such a solution would be a temporary truce. Of course time might result in greater closeness and a willingness to forget or overcome incompatibility. But it's a very big risk, and if you believe that at least part of your motivation in thinking of getting pregnant might be the desire to force your partner to stay in the relationship, it might be a good idea to face up to the possible con-sequences of such an action. If, after all, the break were inevitable, where would that leave you and your child? A clean break between two people whose relationship has been close and loving is hard enough. A break where a child is involved is very seldom clean.

BABY AS AN INTRUDER

When you're pregnant, or thinking of becoming so, it's difficult to think beyond the birth and perhaps the first few years. Some parents can't really envisage a future beyond the first few months, and, as we've seen, they may not even appreciate that those could mean radical changes.

'We were determined not to be dominated by our baby,' one young mother says.

'We saw other couples refusing invitations, never taking a break, having what looked like a really restricted life. Well, the birth was easy, the baby quite a contented one, and we soon resumed our previous habits – the only difference was that we took him with us when we visited friends or went out for the day. That was while he still fitted into his carry-cot and slept most of the time, anyway. By six months it was a different story. He wouldn't settle down except in his own cot. He was upset by any change in routine, and spoilt so many evenings that eventually we decided we couldn't even leave him with a baby-sitter because we'd be called back after we'd been out for an hour or two as he was so distressed. We'd thought of having the kind of holiday we'd always enjoyed – driving and sightseeing. Now that seems quite a crazy idea. So we tend to go out separately, and just stay in at weekends. Perhaps in a year or two we can have a holiday, but it will have to be a different sort of holiday from the kind we prefer – even if he does become more secure and less difficult to manage in strange places. What worries me a lot is the fact that somehow the baby has put a sort of wedge between us. When you can't do things together and you have to give up so much, you begin to find fault with each other and possibly grow apart.'

LIFETIME RESPONSIBILITY Even if you weather the early childhood period relatively easily, the changes in life-style you will have adopted are likely to remain. It's obvious that for many years to come, unless you are rich, or fortunate enough to find yourself in an extended family or communal living situation, your child is going to be your responsibility, shared, if all goes well, with probably only one other adult. If all isn't well, you may find yourself on your own. Whatever the background, though, you'll be tied to this child by the strong bonds of parenthood, and these may never be loosened. As the mother of a grown-up son or daughter, you'll still feel concern about your adult child's health, job, marriage or sexual relationships. You won't intend to interfere in their lives, but you will worry if things go wrong for them. You will delight in their success in personal relations or in their jobs. And a similar concern, perhaps no less intense, will colour your relationship with your grandchildren. There are few parents who, when taking the decision to have a child, aren't taking on a lifetime commitment – 'for better, for worse' in relation to our children is probably something more all-embracing than it is in relation to a marriage partner.

That is what you're really talking about when you ask yourself whether you want to have a baby. Do you want a baby, a toddler, a schoolchild, an adolescent, a young adult and then another generation, perhaps, to be at or near the centre of your life from now until you die? Because that is what it's all about.

PERSONAL EXPERIENCES
The stories of some women and men who have been involved, either as children or parents, in the sort of issues discussed in this chapter may help to illustrate further the points made and perhaps to clarify some of the questions raised. Every individual is different, of course, but you may be able to identify with some of the feelings these people have expressed.

'I think that if I'd really known what difficulties I would face, I'd never have had a child. Our marriage was in trouble, of course, even before I got pregnant, but after the baby was born I was so depressed and exhausted trying to cope with him and the broken nights that I became impossible to live with. My husband showed no sympathy or understanding, and he walked out on us when Rob was only five months old. I'd advise anyone who wasn't absolutely sure of her husband and the relationship not to have a baby: though of course if you think you're strong enough to manage on your own things might be different.'

Or:

'Having a baby was a big decision for me, because I knew absolutely nothing about babies. At first I was quite terrified that I'd drown her in the bath, or that every little snuffle meant she had pneumonia. Later I realised that all new mums feel like this – my health visitor and the local NCT [National Childbirth Trust] teacher were very reassuring and I soon felt much more confident. When I have my next one – if I do – I won't be nearly so anxious.'

Or:

'I've been in a psychiatric hospital for several periods in recent years, suffering from depression. Now my sister has quite unexpectedly become severely depressed after having her baby. I'll have to check with the psychiatrist to see what he thinks about the risk I might run if I had a baby.'

Or:

'My mother certainly wasn't the "perfect" mother, according to the books, anyway. She took only six weeks off when each of her two children were born, we were looked after almost entirely by our grandmother or an aunt, and we really only saw our mother for holidays and at weekends. But she was such fun! She didn't fuss about us making a mess like the mothers of my friends did and she dropped everything when she was with us to talk interestingly about all sorts of things and she took us to unusual places and always had something to say about them. Her friends were lively and stimulating, too. Now that we're grown-up we keep in close touch, because we want to, not out of any sense of duty. She leads her own life and doesn't depend on us in any way. I hope I'll be a mother like that.'

Or:

'I was amazed when I realised, at eighteen or so, that I had actually been an unwanted baby. My parents had never told me that, or given the slightest impression that my arrival had been a bit of a disaster to them – which it had. My mother now tells me that she had the greatest difficulty in accepting me. But she cared for me physically, I suppose, and there's no doubt that eventually she must have done so emotionally, because my memories of our family life are so warm. She confesses now that perhaps they "spoiled" me, as a compensation for the feelings of rejection they'd had when I was a baby. But I hope I haven't suffered from being "spoilt". I just experienced it as love.'

Or:

'From the beginning of my life I've felt unwanted. I was brought up in a children's home and it was a terrible experience. I only hope they're better now. I expect it's because I had the experience that my one aim now is to have children and to give them everything I didn't have. Perhaps I'm being selfish and it's my own need to feel wanted that I have to satisfy. But if I couldn't have children of my own I'd still want to adopt one or two – handicapped or disturbed, it would be a joy to rescue them from being "in care". If only women knew what they do to the babies they have and don't want; people who are against abortion never seem to think of the children.'

Or:

'I'm pregnant and very pleased about it. I don't plan to get bogged down in domesticity, though. I'm lucky because the sort of job I do means that I can work part-time, and my partner works at home. So between us I'm sure we'll manage. If having a baby meant giving up my work I think I mightn't have become pregnant.'

Or:

'How well you cope with the problems with a baby and a toddler seem to me to depend on what sort of network of friends you have. Luckily I have several who have young children of their own. We've helped one another in so many ways. The most important, I think, is that when things get on top of you and you desperately need a few hours off, you can call upon a friend to take over your children, knowing that you'll do the same for her. And when I've had one piece of advice from a health visitor and another from my doctor, my friends encouraged me to use my common sense rather than getting confused by the "experts". Doctors and clinics are useful, of course, but when it comes down to it, it's the support of your friends that helps the most.'

In the next chapter we'll consider the situation of a woman who has the back-up of a partner – man or woman – as well as this support from friends.

CHAPTER 3

A 'STABLE RELATIONSHIP'
YOUR JOINT DECISION?

In this chapter we shall be looking at the situation of the woman who is part of a couple – whether that couple is the conventional married heterosexual one, the increasingly common unmarried heterosexual partnership, or the lesbian partnership – when she is thinking about having a baby. Although in all of these cases there is no certainty that the relationship will last a lifetime, at least at the time when the idea of becoming pregnant begins to fill her thoughts, a woman believes that it will be durable enough to provide two parent figures for her child in her or his early years.

So such couples have a lot more in common with each other than does the single mother with those members of the group who are legally 'single' but in fact expect to live together while their child(ren) grows up. Every mother whose experience is quoted in this book is clear that to be one of a partnership has advantages that outweigh what some perceive as disadvantages – at least where raising children is concerned. As Jean Renvoize demonstrates in her book *Going Solo* (1985), it is perfectly possible to 'go solo' but it isn't always easy – and the views of the single women quoted in the next chapter bear this out.

WILL IT LAST?   We'll look first at heterosexual relationships. In spite of the much-quoted statistic that tells us that one in three marriages breaks down, if you're reading this book the most likely situation is that you'll expect to stay married; after all, two out of three marriages don't end in divorce. And it's fairly *un*likely that, if your marriage seems to be going wrong, you'd be seriously considering having a baby. (Nevertheless, some women whose marriages are in trouble still write to agony aunts with the plea 'don't tell me to have a baby'; their conception of magazine aunties was obviously formed in the 1950s!) And if you're thinking of getting pregnant, you will probably have been married for at least a year – possibly much longer. It follows, then, that you do believe that your marriage relationship is going to last, at least long enough to see you and your child through the first years.

The same applies to a stable relationship which you've entered into and maintained without a marriage certificate. Some would say that in such a relationship there's a greater likelihood of future stability, just because the power-and-possession element inherent in formal marriage isn't operative. The freedom of both partners to go ensures that neither is held against her or his will. This may be a somewhat simplistic view of what is, after all, a deeply emotional situation; but such relationships very often do last at least as securely as the married one. It follows, therefore, that in the absence of other disrupting factors both kinds of relationship can offer a good and secure environment in which to have a child.

This isn't to say that there won't be difficulties, many of which are discussed in detail in later chapters. To decide to have a baby together is something that ideally you won't do until you've raised and thought through a whole number of questions that can materially affect your future.

'IT'S ONLY NATURAL'

But perhaps you've been married for a couple of years, or lived with your partner, or you're pushing thirty. You have good jobs, adequate housing, a future as secure as anyone's can be in the 1980s. You're healthy, and a competent sort of person.

Then the pressure starts. Spoken or unspoken, you feel it, from family, friends, neighbours, the media, 'society'. You even get gripped, sometimes, with an overwhelming urge to have a baby; an urge that seems to come from somewhere inside yourself, that's so strong that you can't believe it's just outside pressure, 'conditioning' or any other convenient explanation for the gut feeling that so unexpectedly overcomes you. It may be primitive, but it can't be denied.

That may be the kind of pressure you can't resist and which will drive you to seek ways and means, in however unpromising a situation, to satisfy it. But if you don't have this feeling, if you believe that but for gratifying the needs of your partner or your parents or because in a vague way it's expected of someone like you, you probably wouldn't have a baby now – or at all – it would seem sensible to weigh up just how much you would be acquiescing in other people's demands; and to decide that in this very important matter a woman does have a right to choose.

Let's look at what happened to some women who took the decision to have a baby without really thinking through the effect it would have on their lives. This is what one of them says:

'We'd been married for three years and we were quite happy together. But by this time both our mothers were dropping hints about their hopes of becoming grandmothers, making us feel we were sort of letting them down by delaying having a baby. My mother kept telling me of old school friends who now had lovely families, showing me photographs of cousins' babies, and so on. They did all look adorable, I must say. Everyone seemed to think we were unnatural, even selfish, not to be wanting a baby, and some people even asked whether there was anything wrong with us. I can't think of any other situation where outsiders would be so nosy about one's private affairs. Of course I can't just blame the people who said these things. The nappy and baby food ads, the write-ups about Princess Di and lots of magazine articles do make having a baby seem not just natural and the right thing to do, but actually a wonderful experience without any snags. You can say we were stupid to fall for all this – but we did. And I do think there's something in the idea that you get broody when you see a lovely baby – I must admit I did. Then my husband – he didn't actually pressurise me but I knew he wanted a baby, not to carry on the family name or anything like that, but because he was like me, he felt we'd be able to bring up a child properly and avoid a lot of mistakes.

'Anyway, we did have a baby. I had a difficult pregnancy – well, that can happen to anyone. The birth was average, I suppose, the usual conveyor belt stuff. We were so looking forward to getting her home, but what we didn't realise was that in hospital, despite all the disadvantages, the main burden of coping with constant crying, colic, wind and other troubles is taken off you. When you get home, it isn't. Brian took a week off work to help, and it was a help. But after that I was more or less on my own during the day. Everything seemed to go wrong. I was exhausted with getting up several times a night and the constant breast-feeding that seemed to be the only way of pacifying the baby. I was never sure that she was getting enough. The house got more and more untidy and dirty. Brian came home to find me in tears more often than not, with piles of washing not done, no food in the house, and the baby still crying. What a contrast with the picture we'd had! Things got so bad that Brian too was overtired and felt that his work was suffering. The only way he could cope was sleeping downstairs every other night, where he wouldn't hear me and the baby. As for sex – forget it, is what I felt.

'Well, of course it couldn't last, and it didn't. A neighbour came to the rescue. Despite the pressure from the clinic to continue with the breast-feeding, she suggested that I should gradually go over to the bottle. I didn't want to, because everyone tells you "breast is best" and I believe them. But she volunteered to give the baby one bottle feed during the day, so that I could sleep, and suggested that Brian would be able to take some nights, too, which of course he couldn't do when the baby was breast-fed.[*] She suggested that until I got straight it was worth spending money on disposables, to cut down on the washing. She offered to do some shopping for me when she did her own. She certainly saved my sanity.

'Well, things did get better, and now the baby is fine – eating and sleeping well, smiling and laughing and doing lots of funny little things that make you feel that it was all worthwhile. But I feel very bitter that no one really prepared me for the difficulties we might face. If I'd known I'd have organised everything much better and made sure of some back-up from at least one other person beside Brian. I'd have realised that for the first few weeks a baby really is a full-time job and other things have to take second place, or have to be done by someone else. It's the feeling that everyone else can cope, that you're a miserable failure, that gets you down.'

FAIR SHARES? 'We truly intended to take fair shares,' reports one young mother.

---

[*] As any baby book will tell you – and your midwife, health visitor and doctor will agree – breast milk is the best milk for a baby. The great majority of women can breast-feed – sometimes with support from a breast-feeding counsellor contacted through the National Childbirth Trust. Even breast-feeding for a few weeks is beneficial to baby and mother, if for some reason it's not possible to continue for longer. But someone whose physical or emotional health makes breast-feeding a cause of severe stress shouldn't be rigid about it. Millions of babies have survived healthily on 'formula' milks.

'He would do the shopping, I would do the cooking. We'd take turns bathing the baby, making up the bottles, cleaning the house, doing the washing. I'd go back to work once my maternity leave was up and we'd find a good child-minder for the baby.

'Well, of course I was at home for the baby's first few months, and it seemed ridiculous to expect Alan to take over his half-share of jobs when I was at home all day and he had been working. So we got into the pattern of Alan "helping" with the baby and the household chores while I did most of the work. It was difficult, almost impossible, to get out of this when eventually I went out to work. Alan did "help" a bit more, but somehow I began to feel I was asking too much of him. He made such a thing of being exhausted after a day's work. In the end he complained if I left him reading the paper in the same room as the baby with the idea that he'd keep an eye on her. We had such rows about who was to do what that I rather feebly gave in. I couldn't cope with a full-time job and everything else, so I went part-time. That's blocked any idea of getting promoted to the job I'd expected. I'll just have to coast along and be thankful I've got *any* job, I suppose.'

This woman feels frustrated and rather bitter, but she can't see any solution until the child is a lot older.

Another mother feels a certain amount of guilt because she *did* ensure that her partner took his full share of responsibility. She hates the idea that the reason for her guilt is primarily because he is the major earner, and that because of this he 'should' be exonerated from domestic jobs. She says:

'It's absolutely against my principles to see things in these cash terms. It's not my fault – or his – that his job is more rewarding in money than mine. And it's not only money, either. Because he's got this job and the status that goes with it I actually feel that he's more *important* than I am, and that I'm holding him back when I expect him to take time off to look after the children if they're ill, or to take his turn at getting up if one of them is restless in the night. I don't approve of myself for thinking like this, but I do!'

It's simple enough in theory to agree that the old pattern of father/breadwinner, mother/housewife isn't for you – as it isn't for the huge numbers of mothers of young children now working outside the home full- or part-time. Economic necessity drives many into low-paid, unsatisfying work; others can't conceive of dropping their interesting and well-paid jobs for a purely domestic existence. So you and your partner decide that the care of your children will be a shared affair; but as we've seen, this is more often decided than achieved.

If 'sharing' is sometimes a sick joke as far as the baby's mother is concerned – she knows she's going to do practically everything, and certainly all the less attractive bits of parenting – the idea can occasionally rebound in an unexpected direction.

'My partner was enchanted with the notion of becoming a father,' says another mother.

'He took an enormous – shall I say *proprietory* – interest in the pregnancy. He intervened almost embarrassingly at the ante-natal clinic, and of course he almost took over the birth. I suppose he is a rather dominating person. It seemed fortunate that he could work flexible hours, and of course it did help a lot that he was there to do shopping and other odd things while I was breast-feeding. But soon I realised that he was actually in charge of me and the baby – not sharing, or participating in her care but actually telling me what to do all the time. As she got older she seemed to prefer him to me – if she woke in the night it was always him she called for, if she hurt herself she rushed to him for attention. It was much more "help" than I expected and certainly more than I wanted. I felt he was suffocating us both. In the end I did the "unpardonable" – I walked out on both of them. You can just guess what everyone said to me and about me, and I do feel terrible about abandoning my daughter to such a dominating and controlling person.'

These stories – and there are many other versions of the same sort of experiences – do call into question assumptions about the possibility of total sharing of responsibility when the parents form a 'nuclear family'. Some women, of course, are very happy to take over the prime tasks involved in caring for children. They see this kind of life as a very worthwhile career, and they wouldn't want a husband or lover to be at all heavily involved. 'He does his job, I do mine,' is the traditional, and to some women completely satisfying way of organising their lives. Like the last woman quoted above, they see too much involvement on the part of the child's father as threatening and demanding. Such a mother may react as strongly as that woman did to the 'redundancy' she felt had been thrust upon her. At the very least 'who does what' can become a power struggle. How that is resolved may demand a very basic reappraisal of the whole relationship – possibly even counselling – if it is not to cause a total breakdown of the partnership.

A UNILATERAL DECISION

The point was made earlier that a majority of couples nowadays take a joint decision to start a family. Sometimes, of course, this decision is taken only reluctantly by one partner – usually the man.

'I'd been married before and already had two children,' says Geoffrey.

'I knew what disruption having a baby in the house can cause. However, before we got married we did discuss having children, and I realised how important it was to Lyn, so I did agree. I think she understood that I really wasn't keen, but she probably hoped that once we had a baby I'd change. To some extent I have. But I still feel that the baby is more her child than mine, and I know that Lyn resents this. I sort of do my duty by the baby; but quite frankly my work is more important to me than family life and I won't sacrifice my career to taking a full share in looking after children. You could call the relationship we have now a sort of uneasy truce. Things are bound to get better, though, when the children get older: I say *children*, because in spite of everything, Lyn wants another.'

As we've seen, even joint decisions don't always work out in practice. Kenneth is another man who is quite frank about it. He explains that although in theory he had accepted that the baby would be looked after equally by both partners, it's a lot more convenient for him to opt out on the grounds that his wife is so much better at the job than he is. He admits:

'Yes, I know I'm exploiting her at the moment. All I can say is that once the baby is older, I've promised to see that she gets the chance to go back to University as a mature student and finish her degree. I think I'll be much better at coping with an older child than a toddler. I'm basically not all that interested in very young children. Sometimes I wonder how Deirdre copes alone all day with that demanding kid.'

David is quite sure that he and his partner made a decision that suited both of them.

'We had a firm agreement right from the start that I wasn't going to get too heavily involved as a father. We agreed that I'd play what you might call the "traditional" Dad's role – help out in emergency, get home in time to say goodnight to the children, take them out on a Sunday morning, that sort of thing. We both accepted that this was how it would be. Some of our friends are surprised, because they go for this sharing business, and they think we're really out of step with the times. *We* think we're being realistic. Look at the way so many couples talk about taking fair shares, but when it comes down to it, it's always the mother who's really responsible, who really does the basic work. I'm amused to watch what happens when a modern family is out together – who wipes noses, spoons food into the baby, comforts a crying child and so on? A lot more than half the time it's the mother; yet on a family outing there's absolutely no reason why Dad shouldn't do his share – or more of it, actually, since she's probably got the children all week.'

The only conclusion that can be drawn from the ideas expressed by these three men – and they are fairly typical – is that any decision made in advance about sharing the care of children has to be based on reality and probability, rather than fantasy, or the hope that somehow characters will change. A woman who really accepts that much of the time she'll be on her own with the child is better prepared for that situation than one who feels completely let down when in the event, promises and fine words come to little or nothing. Some may believe that they ought to continue to work for, and hope for, the day when life will be better organised and parenthood is something fully shared by men and women; but that in their own lives, here and now, they have to be prepared to accept that change is slow. One contribution to the future is to help girl children to be strong, assertive and independent, and to encourage boys to develop into caring gentler people so that future generations will be able to choose far more easily than we can today just how *their* children are to be raised.

It is a truism that children learn by example. Parental behaviour and attitudes are far more potent influences than abstract ideas, exhortations or 'non-sexist' books. 'Role models' in the conventional sense are broken down when mother works outside the home and father takes more than the usual share of childcare – doing some of the more mundane jobs like washing and cleaning rather than concerning himself solely with repairing broken toys or taking his son to a football match.

LESBIAN COUPLES

In *Going Solo*, Jean Renvoize included lesbian mothers living with their partners. Here, however, we are considering the similarities and differences between parents living as a partnership on the one hand, and single parents with no permanent 'living-in' back-up, on the other. There would seem to be much more in common between couples, whatever their sexual orientation, as parents, than between 'legally' single (i.e. unmarried) mothers who have partners of either sex and *de facto* single women who choose to become mothers. The latter group are the subject of the following chapter.

Jean Renvoize's finding, that lesbian partners often make very happy relationships with the child that is by its birth the offspring of one of them, is borne out by an interesting piece of research, published in 1983 by Golombok, Spencer and Rutter. The researchers discovered that most of the children studied had been born into heterosexual households, and that therefore 'the findings cannot be generalised to exclusively and permanently homosexual women who have become pregnant by AID'. Nevertheless, of the mothers 'the great majority had been exclusively homosexual for some years,' and it may therefore be assumed that the 37 children studied, whose ages ranged from 5 to 17 in the lesbian households, had spent most or all of their formative years with mothers who were in relationships with women.

Lesbian mothers seeking the custody of children born when they were married face enormous difficulties in the courts. It is claimed that children need to be able to identify with the parent of the same sex, that they have difficulty in accepting their 'correct' sexual orientation, that they may themselves become homosexual, that they may have social difficulties and experience rejection or persecution by their peers. Although the writers reporting the research point out that since most of the children studied were too young for it to be clear what their sexual orientation would be, there was no evidence that the mothers of the children of either sex were influencing them in the direction of homosexuality. As they point out, it is hardly unusual for the children of *heterosexual* parents to be homosexual.

The research also bears out the experience of most women living in a stable lesbian relationship – 'parenting and housekeeping roles were shared between the two women in most of the lesbian households. However, there was some tendency for the mothers to take a dominant role in the care of their own children.' And, to counter the usual allegations that children in lesbian households tend to be more disturbed than those in the heterosexual-parent family, 'it was concluded that rearing in a lesbian household *per se* did not lead to atypical psychosexual development or constitute a psychiatric risk factor.'

What seems to be important for a child is that his or her parents should be in a good relationship, whatever its sexual orientation. The children of hostile and unhappy parents are much more likely to be emotionally disturbed than those where disagreements and violence never erupt.

Although Alice agrees that there are very many aspects of family life that she, her partner, and her child have in common with heterosexual households, she thinks that there's more than one important difference. 'We don't live in such an enclosed world,' she says.

'We seem to have many more friends who come and go, visit us when they're in London, join with us when we all go out together. I don't see many man-woman couples doing that – or if they do, it's in couples like themselves. My son meets so many friends, women and men, that he's never been nervous about strangers and always seems part of a big family. I think he'll grow up to be much more tolerant as well as confident, accepting people's differences and appreciating individual qualities. I see his life as enriched by the way we live.'

Alice and her partner both work part-time. Her son is quite clear about which of them is his mother, but he sees only slightly more of her than of her partner, and he certainly doesn't see one or other of them doing more of the household chores than her fair share. Alice believes:

'Sexual stereotyping can't possibly be part of his consciousness. I don't know what will happen when he goes to school – he's going to find it quite difficult to accept that other children believe that some things are men's jobs and others, women's. I hope he won't.'

ADJUSTING TO REALITY

Whatever the form of the partnership, to be realistic you do have to consider some sort of blueprint of responsibility that's likely to be workable and not put too much strain on your relationship. Being realistic means that each has to accept that there will be limitations to her or his freedom to live the life hitherto taken for granted. Ambitions on the part of one or both of you may have to remain unfulfilled. In the absence of fully satisfactory child care arrangements with paid help or a nursery place – and in today's world it's probable that this will be your situation – complete dedication to both careers is almost certainly not possible. Until you are a parent (and this applies even to teachers, social workers, nursery nurses and others with experience of children) you really can't appreciate the juggling with your day, the stress of hurrying home to be on time for your child to be handed over, the fatigue of a day that follows a badly broken night. Unless one partner (and of course this can be either of you) sees that for a time it may be necessary to take more than his or her share of the load to enable the other to do more outside the home, life can be a constant battle to get everything done, everything under control, everybody reasonably happy. Better still, of course, if it's possible to accept that, in order to take really equal shares, equal adjustments have to be made. But to achieve this balance finances have to be adequate, and dedication to one's job less important than personal relations.

This equation is reached satisfactorily by many couples, but it's generally as a result of forethought – or a major confrontation when things have gone badly wrong. Muddling along won't work in the long run. Resentments build up, communication ceases and unless the situation can be rescued, the looked-forward-to presence of a child can be the major factor in the ultimate break-up of the partnership.

If pleasure in parenthood and some sacrifice of outside ambitions on the part of both comprise the balance that can be achieved without any real sense of loss or martyrdom, the rewards are enormous. The relationship will become stronger in the shared joy of watching and helping your child grow up as an independent person. This is much more likely to happen to you if you'll accept the need to talk about the future in a realistic way with your partner, discarding rose-coloured spectacles and romantic ideas, but not, on the other hand, exaggerating your own fears and inadequacies and regarding parenthood as something impossibly difficult. Most people believe that a settled, stable background is the best insurance for the future happiness of a child. One way to achieve this – though it's not the only way – is within a home where both parents live together, work together, and care for their child together.

All the evidence so far seems to show that this is far more important than the composition of the family in which the child is to grow up. But now we'll look at the experiences of mothers who have chosen to remain single.

CHAPTER 4

STAYING SINGLE
COULD YOU REALLY GO IT ALONE?

Until quite recently the idea of a single or unattached woman *deciding* to have a baby was regarded as totally outrageous. There were 'unmarried mothers' – now more often described as heading 'one-parent families' – but the perception was that these were women who had become pregnant against their will and had decided to keep their babies rather than having an abortion or choosing adoption. The very few women who had apparently chosen to have children without a permanent male partner were seen as extremely eccentric and irresponsible – unless they were 'names' like Rebecca West.

Although it is still very much of a minority movement, a number of influences have combined to make choosing to have a baby while remaining single considerably more acceptable than it would have been in the past. Those who have done this have often been greatly influenced by feminist ideas and the way in which they see sexual politics; and the 'general public' has become more willing to accept the possibility that single parenthood is a real option by publicity surrounding entertainers and other figures whose 'private lives' are now very much in the public eye. These groups, of course, tend to be middle-class and/or moneyed. Such women are more likely to have their paths eased by their ability to pay for the child care that is so lacking in the rest of society; and their jobs are often such that they can work part-time or adjust their hours to fit in with looking after children. Other women, who decide to become pregnant without a permanent male partner, have a considerably harder time and depend very greatly on traditional family help, which may be less easily available under present conditions than it was in their own mothers' experience.

If you have no permanent partner, and know that you will never have one, this must affect in a most fundamental way your decision about motherhood. Perhaps your background is one in which a high proportion of families are 'headed' by the mother. Aunts, grandmothers, friends are the people you'll look to to share the care of your child, and if you yourself were brought up in this way you'll probably feel that being without a father isn't such a depriva- tion – it could actually be an advantage. Those whose background is the 'nuclear family', though, or who firmly believe that the conventional father/mother/ child family offers the best chance of security and stability, naturally hesitate. It's one thing to run the risk of the child losing her father through death or divorce. Quite another deliberately to have a baby knowing that she'll never have a father.

There's little hard evidence to help a single woman faced with this dilemma. The book *Father Loss* (1985) by Elyce Waterman deals specifically with the effects on girls and women of the absence of a father through death or divorce. The evidence she produces as a result of questioning over six hundred American women about their lives following the loss of their fathers makes somewhat gloomy reading. Most claim that they have never recovered from the loss of their father – it's affected their self-confidence, their ability to make relationships and their feelings about their own children. However, loss of a father who was once part of the couple who produced the child, and, in most cases, someone the girl remembers, may be very different from the situation where the mother has always been single. Unlike the widow or divor- cee, she probably hasn't suffered the shock and trauma involved in becoming unexpectedly partner- less, with its inevitable effects on her daughter. So, although it's worth considering the similarities and differences in the two situations, the book doesn't really answer the question in your mind right now.

As we've seen, and will continue to see right through this book, bringing up a child on your own can be hard. All mothers need a network of good friends as practical and emotional back-up, and none more than the single mother. And, as Jean Renvoize shows in *Going Solo*, most single mothers do seek this help.

The child of the single mother today is not likely to feel isolated and abnormal, as so many of the women in Waterman's book felt they were when they were growing up twenty or more years ago. In most classes at school around one-third of the children will come from homes where there is no permanent father figure. Increasingly we may expect that the children of a lesbian household too will be accepted in the same way, as greater tolerance and a wider variety of life-styles develop.

It's obvious that many women who for a variety of reasons wish to remain single are not, just because of this decision, so unlike other women that they also don't want children. It's all too clear that, no matter what the cultural circumstances, there have always been those who marry, or form permanent relationships with men, simply in order to fulfil this need. They may, or may not, form a good relationship with their partner. If it's not a good one, many women have had to resign themselves to the fact that forming this relationship is the price they have had to pay to fulfil their need for children. Economic dependence plus tradition have brought unhappiness to countless women in the past, and still today these factors play a crucial role in maintaining 'family life.'

A HARD TIME   Personal experiences, added to the ways many perceive their family members and friends to have suffered as a result of being single parents, do play a part in dissuading a majority of women from choosing lone parenthood.

'I was desperately keen on having a baby; I felt that at thirty two if I didn't have one soon it would be too late. I had several men friends whom I liked a lot, but no one I felt close enough to to want to spend the rest of my life with him. I won't go into the details of how I got pregnant, with Tom as the father: but it was fair and above-board, we both knew what we were doing. I took full responsibility for the child, and he was in complete agreement about that.

'Obviously I planned to keep my job after I'd taken the full maternity leave you're entitled to. Everything went quite well, and when the baby was a few months old I went back to work. What I hadn't really understood was the difficulty of coping alone when you're a working mother. There were no nursery places available – it's that kind of borough – and I couldn't afford a private nursery. So it was a question of child-minding. I got names from the council social services department of registered child-minders, but I'm afraid I wasn't much impressed with the first two I visited. The third seemed more the kind of person I could trust with Michael. So I fixed up with her to have him from eight thirty to five thirty every day. He seemed quite happy with her, put on weight and developed normally. But after a few months she got ill, and had to give up. I did find another minder, but Michael doesn't seem to settle well with her – whether she doesn't suit him or whether he's upset by the change, I don't know.

'So now I have a difficult time with him in the evenings and weekends. He won't eat, he grizzles and cries and every morning without fail he clings to me and screams when I leave him. This sort of scene gets me down – I'm upset for the rest of the day. Do I take it too seriously? I don't know. If I had someone to share the problems with it might be easier. You could at least talk things over and work out some kind of scheme for coping. My family's no help at all.

They won't have anything to do with me because of Michael. I could have guessed as much – they're very religious – but I did think that once I had a baby and they actually saw him they'd come round. It's a great grief to me that they won't even see him.

'So the position I'm in is that I have a real problem with Michael and for the first time I'm feeling guilty about what I may have done to him depriving him not only of a father but of grandparents as well. The funny thing is that I did go into this with my eyes open – or so I thought – but it just hasn't turned out as I expected.'

Meg's experience has led her to feel great concern for a friend who is wondering whether to embark on the same venture:

'I can't tell her what to do, of course, but I hope that she'll really think hard before she decides to get pregnant. If you've got supportive friends, parents who'll help, a good job you can go back to when you're ready – that's quite different. Much as I love Michael, if I'd known what a struggle it was going to be, I don't think I'd have had him.'

Sometimes the difficulties friends have in bringing up a child alone do affect the decision a single woman faces when she wonders whether she should have a baby.

'Life at home was very unhappy,' says Coral.

'My parents are very strict and they made all sorts of impossible rules, such as making us be home by ten p.m., forbidding us to have boyfriends and not letting us wear make-up. My sister, who's older than me, got pregnant. Of course she got thrown out of the house and was shown no sympathy whatever. They just didn't want to know what happened to her. Eventually she got a council flat – her boyfriend hadn't had anything to do with her once he knew she was pregnant – so she was absolutely on her own with the baby. And that's the way it's been. She's had a horrific struggle to keep going and look after the baby properly.

'Although a lot of people believe that girls like me get pregnant just so that they can leave home and be given council housing and live on social security I don't think it's true. I have left home – it was difficult to do because I suppose in spite of everything I do love my parents – but I did it because I wanted to be independent of them and everyone else. Seeing how my sister has been forced to live makes me quite certain I'd never want to be a single parent. It's certainly not the bed of roses some people would like to believe. Before I have a baby – and I hope one day I will – I've got to be sure that it's going to have a proper Dad and a proper home to live in. So far that's just a dream.'

Millie is another young woman who has personal experience of being part of a one-parent family:

'My father walked out on us when I was six and my brother was a baby. He was white and my mother is black. She's been a wonderful mother to us. We never went really short of anything, but looking back on it I realise that *she* did. She didn't look after herself properly – for instance, she wouldn't have an operation she needed until I had got through my O-levels.

'The result of her neglecting herself is that her health is now not at all good. She can't work and her social security is pitiful. My brother and I help as much as we can – it's the least we can do – but neither of us is in a good job.

'People are sorry for the children in a one-parent family – deprived and all that. But women like my mother are really the ones who suffer, because what mother would let her children go short if she could help it? She had no choice, she says, and of course in some ways that's true. But I do have a choice, because I'm not married and I don't have a regular boyfriend and until I do I'll never have a baby. Maybe not even then. . . .'

Another woman who has had a rather different experience is Sheila. She had an abortion at nineteen, and remembers it as a nightmare, not because of the abortion itself but because of the way she felt afterwards:

'I didn't expect to feel anything much, but when I was pregnant although it was a real shock because my boyfriend had been using a sheath, in one way I felt rather pleased. I liked the feeling of having a baby inside me. But it just wasn't sensible to go on with the pregnancy – I was studying and I had nowhere to live, and no money. I didn't see myself coping as a single parent, because I didn't want to stay with the boyfriend and really I had no one else to help me out. I was lucky to get an NHS abortion and it was all over very quickly. What I didn't expect was that I felt really cheated afterwards. I got very depressed and actually I had to drop out of the course I was doing because I couldn't cope. Silly, really, when it seemed at the time that I'd made a sensible decision. But I've found out now that a lot of girls do feel like that after an abortion.

'I've more or less got over it now. And in a way I'm pleased I had the experience of being pregnant even though it had to end as it did. I look forward to being pregnant again, and keeping the baby; but I'll make sure I don't ever put myself in the position where I might have to have another abortion. I couldn't go through it a second time.'

RECIPE FOR SUCCESS

All the women quoted so far in this chapter decided either that they made a mistake in 'going solo' or that, based on the experience of other women, they wouldn't risk single parenthood. But what about the women who have made the choice, and are happy about it? The stories of many such women are recounted in Jean Renvoize's book, and a good proportion of the mothers quoted in Stephanie Dowrick and Sibyl Grundberg's book *Why Children?*, too, are single and feel that they made the right choice. What is noticeable and noteworthy about all of them is their feminism, something that has a crucial bearing on the way they live their lives. Many of the women interviewed by Jean Renvoize, were, as we saw, not strictly 'single', because they lived in lesbian partnerships. Others were lesbians without long-term partners; and of the rest who felt that motherhood had been right for them (and not all did) most lived in shared housing where they could expect – and got – a great deal of back-up from their friends. These situations are very different from that of the 'average' single mother attempting, like Meg, to go it alone with her child.

Of all the women whose experiences have been quoted so far, Sonia is perhaps the one who gave the greatest thought to her situation before becoming pregnant. Now in her late thirties, and single, she says that like most young women she had always believed that 'one day' she would have a child. But when, some years ago, she became accidentally pregnant, her circumstances, and the nature of her relationship with the man involved, were such that she decided to have an abortion – something that she has never regretted.

It was later that, as she says, her sexuality was changing and she recognised that she was a lesbian. She also became more aware than ever that she really wanted a child – and more determined to make sure that if she had one she should be living in reasonable comfort and security, with support from other women and men to enable her to give the child the sort of background which she believed essential. All her working life she had been involved with children and she felt that stability was something that every child needs in her or his early life. She took a secure job, and got a mortgage on a shared house, before considering pregnancy.

'Of course I could have got pregnant as the result of a casual encounter or AID [Artificial Insemination by Donor] through an agency or self-insemination. I did consider these options. But I felt that somehow they were not for me. I felt I wanted to know and respect the father of my child, that it should be someone with whom, if possible, the child could have some sort of relationship.'

Sonia realised that these conditions were indeed very difficult to fulfil. She considered, and rejected, the possibility of asking several men she knew whether they would fill this role. Then, when she discussed her dilemma with an old and close friend, to her surprise the friend suggested that her own partner might be willing to father Sonia's child. She says:

'He was someone I had certainly thought of, but I had totally dismissed the idea because of his relationship with my friend. Their partnership seemed a very stable one; they have children of their own. But I couldn't possibly have considered seriously asking him. I don't think many relationships are secure enough to stand up to such a possible threat.'

Sonia says that she considered the suggestion seriously only because it had come from her friend herself. Further thought on the part of all three adults involved resulted in an agreement that Sonia and her friend's partner (whom Sonia had actually known for some years) should have intercourse with the intention of Sonia becoming pregnant by him; that if she did, he would maintain an involvement with the child and that the child – and the couple's family – would acknowledge his paternity.

The months that followed were a great strain, Sonia admits. She and her friends live in different cities, a hundred miles apart. Sonia had to keep a careful record of her menstrual cycle, so that she could have intercourse with the potential father at the right time of the month. As she was working, it was far from easy to arrange meetings in one or other city just at her most fertile time. Several months passed without success. For a few months she gave up the idea. Then she decided on a few further 'tries' – and after nearly two years since making the decision she became pregnant.

Throughout her pregnancy Sonia had the practical and emotional support of friends, including those with whom she shared her house, and at the birth no fewer than three were present – somewhat to the surprise of the hospital staff, because the man amongst them was not the father, and the party was rather larger than usual.

Since the birth of her son, Sonia has seen his father several times, and his other children have enjoyed meeting the baby. When they're a little older the relationship will be explained to them, and Sonia's son will be made aware that her friend is his father. The relationship between the partners hasn't been adversely affected in any way, Sonia believes. She sees her woman friend's initiative as a truly loving gesture towards her – a sisterly act. 'I'm incredibly lucky to have such good friends,' she says.

Sonia admits that she's someone who seldom acts without a great deal of thought, and though she wouldn't take it upon herself to advise anyone else how to run her life, she feels it's important for someone contemplating single parenthood to think things through very carefully.

'I had to have a secure job to which I could return after having the baby. I had to have friends to help me and share some of the pleasure and responsibility at home. I had to have good living conditions. It was only when I was fairly certain about all that that I went ahead. Even so, there was the worry that I might never get pregnant – but that can happen to anyone.'

ARTIFICIAL INSEMINATION

In recent years a number of single lesbian women have, like Sonia, decided to become pregnant. They have planned to become mothers, through an arrangement with a man they know, who may, indeed, be a dear friend, or through artificial insemination, using the sperm of a known male, employing a simple self-insemination technique. Once this method is understood, there is no need to employ doctors or commercial agencies – unless, as in one much-publicised case in the United States, you want to select a 'genius' as the father of your child, or you know absolutely no male who would be willing to donate his sperm.

The AIDS (Acquired Immune Deficiency Syndrome) scare has meant that women considering artificial insemination may think about the advisability of ensuring that any partner or donor has had a blood test to make sure that he is free of the virus. A few babies whose parents have AIDS have been affected, and it's possible that there will be more. This, of course, applies equally to heterosexual relationships, since we know that it's by no means only gay men who are affected. Until recently, gay men have provided a common source of donated sperm.

Later in this book there's a discussion about AIDS and how it might affect anyone thinking of artificial insemination (see pages 92–3).

There are problems and difficulties that a lesbian woman or a lesbian couple can face from the medical establishment when they wish to become mothers without the active participation of a man. This is where a self-insemination group can provide practical, non-judgmental help.

The majority of women in a self-insemination group are single women – heterosexual or lesbians without a regular partner. One running in the London area has produced a booklet obtainable from the Women's Reproductive Rights Information Centre (see page 180 for the address).

Annie is a member of this group, and she explains how it works.

'Some of the donors are friends or friends' lovers. But there can be problems – in some cases the donor wants involvement, or greater involvement than the woman is prepared to welcome. A woman who would prefer to have sole care and responsibility for her child born by AID would do better to arrange to use the sperm of an unknown donor. We have been able to arrange this in some instances. We advertise quite regularly in *City Limits* and we've had some considerable response. When someone replies, he's sent a very full questionnaire, covering all physical aspects – height, hair and eye colouring, etc as well as his medical history and questions about hereditary conditions. We also ask about his racial origin – that can be important to some women, black or white – and ask him for any other relevant information about himself. We also want to know that he's had the HIV (human immunodeficiency virus) tests with written confirmation that he's clear. We tell him that both he and the woman being inseminated will remain totally anonymous, so that there's no question of his turning up later and demanding access to the child. If he, and our conditions, are acceptable, matters are arranged through a go-between.'

WRRIC (see page 180) can give information about this and other self-insemination groups, and AID can be arranged through the British Pregnancy Advisory Service and a Harley Street clinic.

THE 'ONE-PARENT' FAMILY

So where does this leave the single parent? Earlier we looked at the experience of Meg who tried to go it totally alone, and who found life with a baby or toddler extremely difficult. There are organisations that can offer help and advice and in some places, local groups where single parents can get together and support each other in many different ways. Again, having sufficient money to pay for back-up services can make all the difference. A single mother can, of course, decide that for a few years she won't be able to work outside her home. This solves the problem of child-minding, but it certainly doesn't solve financial problems. Living on social security is far from easy. Not only will mother and child have to go without things that most people would consider as necessities, but any idea of affording so-called luxuries – like a night out with friends or a decent holiday – has to be jettisoned.

If, like very many women, you want a child but you don't want a permanent partner, this is a possible option – difficult, as we've seen, but in some circumstances perfectly viable. If you can afford to give your child everything she needs in terms of care and nurture, if you have a good, supportive social circle, what will she miss? The convention is that a child needs a role-model but also to understand the role of the opposite sex. How valid is this idea? You may well believe that a little boy would not be the kind of child you'd hope for if he modelled himself on the sort of men you know! And how good a start in life would it be for a daughter to live in a family 'headed' by a dominant and dominating man? Could it be better for a child of either sex to grow up with the model of a strong, independent woman – you – rather than absorb the ideas, values, attitudes and behaviour commonly accepted as the norm in the conventional family set-up?

The problem of single motherhood may be less in its effect upon the child than the difficulties the situation can create for *you*. As we've seen, when things go wrong – the baby is ill, the toddler is overactive, the older child is in trouble at school – it's very helpful to be able to share the worries, and in many cases the best person to share them with will be a partner. Conventionally, the partner will be the child's father, who might be expected to take a greater responsibility for her than anyone else, and to care much more about the outcome of any difficulty than someone unrelated to her. Experience tells us, however, that this is very often not what happens. 'Management' of children is left to their mother, and the father's intervention, when it occurs, may be ill-considered, damaging and aggressive. Many women – married or unmarried – find far greater support and positive help from relatives and friends. Their own mothers may offer wisdom and a helpful degree of detachment from the day-to-day problems. Good friends, especially those with children of their own, can provide a sounding board on whom to try out various ideas and work out possible solutions. You needn't feel you're imposing on them – you'd do the same for them, and probably will.

THE FATHER'S RIGHTS?

There's one aspect of single parenthood that may, quite reasonably, worry anyone contemplating having a baby on her own. That is, that despite all his assurances to the contrary, the child's biological father may later claim a share in her upbringing. There have been cases – Polly Toynbee reported one in the *Guardian* in 1986 – where for some obscure reason a man who has quite happily waived all claim to his baby during the mother's pregnancy and while the baby was very young, has suddenly changed his mind and demanded access. 'Access', unfortunately, is often interpreted by the courts as more than just permission to visit the child (which some mothers are quite willing to agree to). It can mean that, just as a divorced father is frequently allowed to have his child on weekend or holiday visits, while she spends most of her time with her mother, a man who is agreed to be the father of an 'illegitimate' child may also be able to have her to stay with him.

The courts may see a mother's refusal to allow this not as a desire to protect her child from bewilderment and disruption but as over-possessiveness or bloody-mindedness. Magistrates aren't always well versed in child psychology and will often see a man's rights as a father as more important than the wishes of the mother or the welfare of the child.

It is possible that if the mother arranged for her former partner to state in writing that he waived all claim to see or share in any way in the upbringing of the child, before the birth, this would negate any future claim on his part. Since no one can ever be totally sure that there can never be a change of mind on the part of someone else, this step may be worth serious consideration. The situation would be less clear-cut if the mother were anxious – as Sonia was – to maintain contact with the father; or if she felt hesitant to raise the matter because she was convinced that the difficulty would never arise.

Anyone worried about the possibility, however remote, that her child's father might later lay claim to access and regular contact, or who experiences such unexpected claims, could seek advice from the National Council for One-Parent Families (see pages 178–9) or the Rights of Women custody worker. A high street solicitor may well wish to do the best for his client, but, like many magistrates, could be biased in favour of fathers and might not understand a mother's motivation, mistaking her anxiety and concern for vindictiveness towards her child's father. Until all such matters come within the jurisdiction of a Family Court – something the government has so far refused to set up – disputes will be handled by people who have no understanding of children and their needs. For information on the present legal position of 'illegitimate' children, see the Appendix (page 172).

Every 'single' mother interviewed for this book agreed that the availability of help and back-up was crucial. Many emphasised over and over again that they just couldn't have managed their complicated lives without at least one other adult to help take the strain. An experienced midwife, however, does take a different view.

'I don't think all single parents' reactions are negative,' she says.

'There are many women who choose single parent-hood and enjoy it. Of course they have problems, but in my experience, they often feel that they have *less* to deal with than women who are in relationships. The latter have the added problem of dealing with another adult's needs and emotions.

'Many of these women wouldn't call themselves feminists, but still have a strong consciousness about making this step as women on their own. I think there's a class difference here, too. It's more common for working-class women to be, and often to choose to be, single parents. Also there are growing numbers of very young women who choose to carry on with a pregnancy alone, rejecting abortion, adoption and marriage, as a bid for independence. So often these women are looked upon as problems. I believe the majority manage very well and often form their own support groups.'

The next chapter considers the vital question of responsibility and sharing of child care.

CHAPTER 5

SHARED CARE
WHAT DOES IT COST IN TIME, ENERGY, MONEY?

We've looked at some of the reasons why you may still be hesitating about your decisions. Now it's time to think about some practical points that may serve to tip the balance. How to implement them we'll discuss in chapter 8.

WHO WILL BE RESPONSIBLE? Every baby's carer, at least in the very early days, tends to be the mother. But this is to take a fairly limited view of what *caring* involves. Feeding, changing, bathing, comforting – these are necessary, basic forms of care, and not all of them need to come exclusively from the mother. However, if most of them do devolve upon her, there has to be someone else responsible for caring for *her*. As we saw from the stories of women quoted in earlier chapters, motherhood without adequate support can be a lonely and daunting experience.

Emotional back-up, taking over some of the usual household chores, and a genuine sharing of the day-to-day work involved in looking after a young baby are one aspect of the new mother's needs. They're part of the practical kinds of help with which at least one other adult needs to be involved. There's the financial aspect too. Even on maternity pay and with the possibility of returning to outside work after a few months, many new mothers feel a sense of insecurity without their regular pay-slip – and in any event, someone has to help with the short- and long-term expenses incurred in having a baby.

All this demands commitment – both to the mother and to the child. In most cases, this commitment will come from the child's father – just one reason why the decision to have a baby is ideally a joint one. Whether or not the couple are formally married, the majority of people thinking of becoming parents do take this commitment very seriously. It's hard to predict what may happen to any relationship in the future, but at least for the immediate time ahead they plan to stay together, and share, as far as they can, responsibility for the child; supporting each other, making decisions jointly, and providing as good an environment as they can, in physical, emotional and financial terms. How to work this out in practice is a very individual thing, but in pointing out some of the pitfalls and seeing how some couples have avoided them, perhaps we can produce a few guidelines.

A stable home and background for the baby does not, in some cases, necessarily involve the parents' decision to maintain a stable relationship between themselves. Increasing numbers of women see no reason to deny themselves the experience of mother-hood because they aren't willing to commit them-selves to long-term involvement with a man. This is a considered, well-thought-out position, not to be taken lightly or on impulse. As we've seen, the decision to have a baby without a continuing relation-ship with its father need not mean that the woman has to go through the pregnancy and birth and bringing up the child quite alone. A lesbian couple who decide that one is to have a child can share the responsibility for that child in exactly the same way as a heterosexual couple. If one goes out to work, the other may take fuller responsibility for the baby, whether or not she is the actual mother, or the roles can be exchanged if at any time this seems more appropriate. A woman alone can find that close friends, a mother or sister may provide the commitment and care that the woman and her child both need. Groups of friends – women or mixed-sex – may set up house together and share the care of several children. Communal living of this kind is not without problems, as anyone with experience of it will testify: but it does provide children with a background of involvement with several adults other than the mother, and there are children who benefit from this, while the mothers can expect help in crises and group support at other times.

AGREE TO AGREE

Whichever way you decide to organise your life, the decision about ultimate responsibility is so important that it's one to be taken very seriously. Failure to be realistic on this vital point probably wrecks more relationships than any other factor.

'I was like a child wanting a new toy,' says Lucy:

'I really didn't think beyond the first few weeks, the idea of showing off a new baby, all the cosy togetherness and everything – that appealed to me. I wasn't going to go back to work – not me! I was going to stay at home and be a proper housewife and mum. We just didn't discuss how we'd manage without my money, and I really didn't sit down and think how I'd feel, stuck out in this estate all day with no one to talk to, once the novelty had worn off.

'Jimmy was no help. Although he did make some effort to do odd things in the house he did them so badly that I couldn't stand it, and that made him get mad at me for being "ungrateful". He didn't seem to want to change from doing everything he'd always done before. I used to go with him when he went fishing on Sundays – with a baby, how could I? So he went alone. He kept on going out with his workmates for a drink on Friday evenings – I'd done the same with the girls in the office, but of course that's finished now, so I spent Friday evenings alone. We had rows about this and the result was that he stayed out other nights, too. I know I handled it all badly; I should have been able to accept that once you've got a baby, things are bound to change. And I was so boring, I should think that would have driven him away, even if we hadn't rowed. Being so hard up didn't help, either. Anyway, in the end he walked out on us, and I'm getting a divorce.'

Jennie and Philip were much more realistic in their planning. Philip's sister had three children and they'd seen, as they say, 'How not to do it.' Before making up their minds to try to have a baby they tried to foresee possible problems and how they might be dealt with. Jenny explains:

'We both had interesting jobs, and neither of us wanted to give up work for any length of time. We wanted to bring up the baby ourselves, perhaps with just a little outside help, and that meant that one or both of us would have to consider changing the way we worked. We talked it over, and in the end we decided that Philip's situation was more flexible than mine. He could work part-time at home, building up a small business, while I'd go back to my job after my maternity leave. We decided to put this plan to the test as soon as possible, so that there'd be some experience of how it would work before we started the baby. For a couple of months we had to live on my earnings while Philip got started, then the cash flow was eased and although he didn't make as much as he'd done in a regular job, it was enough. Then we could carry out the rest of our plan; I got pregnant and during that time we arranged that a neighbour with her own toddler would have the baby for one day a week so that Philip would be free to go out and get business and make contacts.

'Everything's fine. I leave the house at nine every morning with the breakfast washed up and the bed made and the baby fed. Philip does a bit of house-work, then settles down to work with an ear cocked for the baby. He stops work for a couple of hours during the day – longer if the baby needs him – then does another hour or so before I get home. I take over the baby completely while Philip gets the meal – he likes cooking. After the baby's in bed and we've had our supper, Philip sometimes has to do a bit more paperwork and I may do odd jobs like ironing. But we do have some evenings together; and we go out once a week when my mother comes to baby-sit. The arrangement with the neighbour works out OK, too. We pay her a reasonable amount for the days she has the baby.

'I won't say we aren't sometimes rather rushed and tired – but it's worth it. If the business continues to do well we may either arrange to have more child-minding or else Philip will employ someone to help him. Meanwhile I do intend to carry on with my job – as a result of the way we've planned things I can concentrate on it without worrying about what's happening at home, and that's paid off in every way.'

Not every couple is as fortunately placed as Jennie and Philip – but most can do something to anticipate possible difficulties and frictions, and try to adapt their way of life so that the whole burden of child care doesn't fall on one person; and the whole burden of earning the money doesn't fall on the other. That seems to be the best way of dividing responsibility, in any couple situation.

When it's the woman who works at home the problem may be trickier. Conditioning makes it hard for her to opt out of child care while she gets on with her job. Perhaps a rearrangement of both partners' timetables, flexitime, a part-time playgroup or paid help for a few hours a day might provide solutions. But priorities do have to be worked out in advance, especially as a toddler can be much more demanding of a home-based worker's time than a young baby.

WHAT ABOUT YOUR WORK?

There's been a trend in recent years for women to have their planned babies several years later, on average, than did women of an earlier generation. This is partly because of better contraception, making reliable planning possible, but also because many women believe that it's better to take a break from their jobs or careers after they've built up a record that will make it easier to get or retain a good job afterwards. At that time, too, income is more likely to be adequate to allow for savings, equipping the baby, and other foreseeable expenses. All this makes timing quite important, but at which point you decide to 'retire' for a while must be an individual matter. If you waited until you reached the top of your particular tree, you might be too old to conceive easily or go through a pregnancy safely. Once more, it's a question of balancing how much you want a baby, whether your job or career is important enough to defer pregnancy – bearing in mind that there *are* some risks involved in leaving it beyond the mid-thirties.

Most women with jobs they want to return to will probably feel they've got enough experience and knowledge by the time they've been working for a few years – which will bring them to the age of about twenty-five to thirty-three. By that time you'll probably know how important your job is to you, what the career structure is, and whether or not you'll care about the possibility that you'll stay at your present level of income and responsibility. And in many ways, this is the ideal age to have a baby – you have the maturity to know your own mind and to cope with problems, plus the health and energy to meet the demands of motherhood.

But just how feasible is it to make plans to return to work after a short break? Many thousands of women do this, of course. Many more would do so if there were more opportunities for part-time work or job-sharing. But there's no denying that the toll on women who attempt to go out to work, give adequate attention to a baby and shoulder most of the housework, is enormous. Until we organise things better, until partners do more than offer token help, for the majority of women this situation will continue. A major problem for the vast majority of these women is child care, and we'll look at the options.

WORKER, MOTHER OR BOTH?

On pages 169–72 there's a rundown on legislation affecting women who leave work temporarily, late in pregnancy and for a few months thereafter. If you have been working for a large organisation your position should be secure. In the same section there is information on statutory grants and allowances. Just make sure you comply with current regulations regarding notice of ceasing work, stating your intention to return, and giving notice when you intend to do so.

The question still remains, though – in your circumstances how feasible is this plan? It's a hard fact of life that many women have found the problems of child care virtually insurmountable. And a few, despite earlier intentions, decide that after all they are so delighted with the experience of motherhood, and believe so strongly that their presence is important to the baby, that they will stay at home, at least for the first few years.

However, let's assume that you do plan to return to work outside the home. Have you looked into the availability of child-minding, day nurseries, neighbourhood schemes, paid help of various kinds? Do you know how much it will cost to have your baby cared for during your working day? Your probable income may be sufficient to cover the cost – with or without leaving anything over and above what you have to pay out. (Some women think it's worthwhile to retain their jobs even if they 'make' nothing out of working.) On the other hand, if your work is low-paid you could find it would actually cost you so much more than your earnings to have your child cared for that it just wouldn't make sense. So it's sensible to find out about the local costs. In chapter 8 there's a more detailed discussion about child care options, from private nannies to child-minders to day nurseries to help from neighbours.

Perhaps, like Jennie and Philip, whose arrangements were described earlier in this chapter, you can work out a good scheme for genuinely shared care with your partner to enable at least one of you to work outside the home. But if for any reason you feel that this isn't going to happen in your case, it may be that the decision whether or not to have a baby – or when – will depend very largely on the arrangement *you* can make for your baby to be well looked after while you work.

WHEN PLANS GO WRONG

You may do all your homework and your plans for child care may seem watertight, but – as some of the women quoted earlier found – circumstances can change or you may find that your plans were unrealistic. If you possibly can, it would seem a good idea to think about a possible back-up arrangement to meet an emergency or a longer-term disruption of your life. This might not be anything as dramatic as a walk-out on the part of your partner – though this does happen – but have you thought what you would do if you, your partner or your child-minder were to become ill?

Jan's arrangements were going reasonably well – her son was looked after by his grandmother the three days a week Jan was working, and as the grandmother lived nearby it was very convenient for Jan to leave him at her house or for the grandmother to come to theirs. But when the older woman had to go into hospital for a major operation, and there was a prospect of a prolonged convalescence making it impossible for her to have the little boy for at least six months, Jan was in a fix. Her husband's job took him abroad for weeks at a time, so he couldn't be relied upon to take over any regular responsibility. All that

Jan could do was to take her annual holiday so that she could be at hand while her mother was in hospital and meanwhile to search desperately for a solution to her problem.

She was just about to give up and resign from her job when she came to a fairly satisfactory arrangement. The child was just old enough to be accepted at a playgroup – mornings only. Like most playgroups, this one was run largely by the children's parents, so of course Jan was expected to take her turn at the group. She was able to do this because she had two non-working days a week. And she found another playgroup mother, who wasn't going out to work, to have the little boy for three afternoons, while she looked after the other child for the remaining two plus the odd weekend day or baby-sitting evening. So Jan was able to keep her job after all – but at the cost of a lot of worry and complicated arranging. If she'd been less keen on her job and less resourceful about finding alternative care for her child, she could have been defeated. She's still dependent, as she says, on the other mother's willingness and ability to keep up the arrangement – and playgroup holidays do present a problem.

It's too much to expect that you'll be able to foresee and guard against every possible contingency – but it is worth considering what you would do if things didn't turn out as you expect, and how much it would matter to you or your partner if you had to admit defeat for a while and radically change your plans. Failing to make satisfactory arrangements and to stick to the plans you do make needn't spell permanent defeat. You may have to take two steps backward in order to take one step forward when your child is a little older.

One mother whose plans went wrong had to do just that. She was delighted to get a job in her own profession some distance away from her home. Her elder child was at school, and she was able to make arrangements for after-school care for this child; the younger, two years old, would be able to accompany her mother on the daily drive to work, because there was a workplace day nursery where she could be looked after during working hours.

The little girl didn't settle in very well, and at first her mother thought that it was just a question of the newness of the situation, and that all would soon be well. But in fact things got worse. There were scenes of distress every morning, the child came home even more upset than when she had arrived at the nursery. She went off her food, was more often than not apparently unwell. Once she was able to get a better idea of what was going on in the nursery, the mother became aware that the children were being left far too much to their own devices. Toys were broken or non-existent; staff didn't organise any activities for the children and only intervened in fights and quarrels when blood was shed. She tried to get matters changed – making herself unpopular in the process – and to interest other mothers in the running of the nursery, but with little success.

'I should have been able to do something positive, and I feel rather bad about that. If I'd had the time, maybe I could have got people together. But I had this long journey every day, and had to rush home for the other child. And of course the worst thing was that my little girl was so miserable. How could I let that go on? After three months I just had to resign from the job. I couldn't have my daughter suffering, however much I wanted that job.'

Three years later, with both children at school, she and her husband were able to work full-time, with a 'flexitime' arrangement that enabled each to be with the children for part of each day.

Evidence from research shows that, in general, the children of working mothers don't suffer any real deprivation. There's actually some evidence to show that emotional disturbance can result from a mother's frustration and isolation when she stays at home looking after children when she would prefer to be working outside the home. But these are generalisations. And anyone planning to return to work after she has a child or children does have to consider the possibility – however remote – that her particular child may be one who, for some reason, is extremely dependent on the consistent presence of one person in her life. Of course this need not be the mother: but as things are at present, she's the most likely person on whom this demand may fall.

The child may be physically handicapped, or delicate, or emotionally fragile. No one knows what factors go into the make-up of any individual. No one can predict what the impact of inconsistent or insecure child care arrangements might be on a sensitive child. It's easy to look at other people's children and say either that they're perfectly happy and thriving under whatever system of child care has been arranged for them – or that the reason why they seem awkward, over-demanding or miserable is because they've been wrongly handled: and *we* would do better.

Celia has two children. The elder took quite happily to nursery school and then to the infant school; Celia was able to arrange that another mother took turns with her in having the children for a couple of hours after school so that each mother could do a part-time job. She took two years off to have a second child. She explains:

'I don't like the idea of babies and very young children being in nurseries or with child-minders. But having had no trouble beyond the normal hassles with my first child, I assumed that Ellie would be quite OK with the same sort of arrangement. She wasn't. And then, while she was still unsettled and upset I had to change my working hours. I'd have lost my job if I hadn't been willing to work almost full-time.

'Maybe it's just an unfortunate coincidence, but Ellie just doesn't seem to be able to take the sort of care arrangements we've been able to make for her.

Her response – or so it seems – is that she's always ill.
Since she's been at school – she's seven now – she's
hardly had two consecutive weeks without illness.
This has put a great strain on all of us. I or her father
have to drop everything to stay with her when she's
unwell. She's clearly so miserable when she's left
with other people, however kind they are. The
doctors can find nothing wrong with her – a low-
grade infection is all they can come up with. Now
we're faced with a real dilemma. The easy way out
would be for me to give up work – though that would
be a huge disappointment to me and put us under
some financial strain. But would it really solve the
problem? I'd do anything to help her over this and
giving up my job would be really worthwhile if I were
sure it would be the answer.

'Other people don't have these problems, and that
makes us feel we've mishandled her in some way.
That adds to my guilt – perhaps I shouldn't have put
my career before my family, as I seem to have done.
Ellie turns the knife in my wound when she apolo-
gises for being such a nuisance. But a friend suggests
she's just manipulating us. But then I ask myself why
should she? Again it comes down to – "where did we
go wrong?"'

With hindsight Celia might now say that if only
she'd taken Ellie's particular temperament and needs
into account and had made good arrangements for
her care with just one concerned and loving adult
who would have played a crucial part in the child's
life, Ellie's physical symptoms of inner insecurity and
distress might never have been manifest. The lesson,
perhaps, is that in making plans for the future, a
parent should always take into account the possibility
that for their particular child what works for others
won't work for her. Some just don't have the choice:
circumstances dictate that they're powerless to be
flexible. If you need to work because you need the
money, then you just have to do the best you can for
your children. And if you have the energy to spare,

you might join with others in trying to improve the situation for the children of working mothers. No one knows what the ideal arrangement for any particular child might be – but if there were at least options open to parents in arranging for the care of all kinds of children solutions would be easier to find.

A woman like Celia may be in a better position than many to be flexible. If she gives up her job now, or reverts to part-time working, she'll damage her career, but not disastrously. She believes passionately that a woman has the right to choose to work or not to work – 'It's just in practice that it may not be so easy as it looks in theory,' she says.

WHAT DOES A BABY COST?

'I read somewhere that a child can cost its parents £70,000 to bring up,' said Carol in 1986.

'I didn't believe it – I thought that must be a figure arrived at for rich people wanting private education and lots of luxuries for their children. But now I'm pregnant I realise it may not be so far off the mark. Bob and I have been horrified at the cost of everything we need for the baby. We've had several shopping trips to Mothercare and big stores, and right away decided we'd have to have most of the big items second-hand. We'll paint and renovate them ourselves. We reckon to get an old cot, a pram, a pushchair and a playpen for about £50. These items alone would cost much more than four times as much if we bought them new. But I don't fancy a second-hand mattress, though I'll be glad to have some used baby clothes from friends if they're not keeping them for a second baby. Altogether we've spent £50 on things we had to have new – the absolute minimum, in the hope that presents will make up a bit more. But I realise that a lot of these things are going to be outgrown or worn out in a few months, and from then on, there'll be regular replacements. My sister-in-law tells me she has to spend £15 or £20 for school shoes for her older children, and they last no time at all. Spread over the sixteen, eighteen or twenty years you are responsible for keeping your child, £70,000 isn't out of the way, though it sounds a terrible lot compared with our annual income now.'

Education may be free, but there are always extras – extra curricular activities, holidays and outings – to be considered as the child gets older.

If you decide to look after the child yourself there will be loss of earnings. If you decide to keep on your job, there's the cost of child care. On page 120 we suggest current weekly costs at various forms of care, from private nannies to day nurseries, and in chapter 8 the various options are discussed in some detail.

Most women who desperately want a baby won't be deterred by the prospect of future costs. But it does seem sensible to consider whether you should put off the decision for a few years, or whether you could modify your life-style, change your jobs, share your house or in some other way make it easier to manage your money so that having a child won't be a crippling financial burden. No one can insure against unemployment or misfortune, but having some degree of security about the future does make the decision easier.

Jennie and Philip, quoted above, did work things in such a way that their income was only slightly reduced and their extra expenses minimised. Most prospective mothers, faced with the sort of initial expense involved in equipping a baby, will think as Carol did, in terms of second-hand cots, prams and other basics – and may well have savings to fall back on for these items. Liz and her partner did better than that: very early in their relationship they decided they were going to have a baby a few years ahead, and from then on they saved every penny of Liz's salary.

'It's meant going a bit short, having to be careful. We couldn't have the kind of holidays we were used to, couldn't go out for a casual drink and so on. But it's done two things: it's meant that we could buy everything we needed for the baby and furnish his room from scratch. And it's meant that we were completely used to living on one salary, so it wasn't nearly such a shock when I gave up work as it would have been if our money was suddenly halved. I may go back to work part-time when the baby's a bit older, but there won't be much pressure about it. And when I do get a job the money will be a sort of bonus. I might work for a bit and save money again, and then have another baby. It's forward planning that does it!'

Liz was young enough to be able to put off the start of her family for a few years – she recommends her tactics to anyone in her twenties wanting to have a baby one day.

NOT ENOUGH ROOM?

People living in one room do have babies, of course. But it's an extremely uncomfortable and often distressing experience – one to be avoided if at all possible. One child in a two-roomed flat can be managed more easily if you turn one room into a bed-sitter with the other for the child and her belongings. Many couples can live like this – particularly if there's easy access to outside play space – until their child is older, or there's a second baby. Then things can become difficult. Limited space imposes stress on adults and constraints on a young child that can be really damaging. It's a terrible indictment on our society that so many have to lead such constricted lives – and that to some, even just two rooms to themselves would be an almost unimaginable luxury.

If you are in a position to choose, though, you may decide before starting a baby that you ought to have more space. A move, whether to rented or owner-occupied housing, can be an extremely costly business. If you're reckoning up the cost of having a child you'll have to take this into account. Increased rent or mortgage, legal fees, moving expenses, increased outgoings, higher cost of decorations and repairs, new furniture and furnishings – estimate these and tot up the figures and you may be horrified. Think, too, of possible extra cost of travel to work. Of course there may be compensations in addition to the extra space – a pleasanter environment, perhaps, or nearness to work, family and friends.

But could any extra space be created in your present house or flat? Conversions and additions, though very expensive, may still be much cheaper than a move, in the long run. The advertisements for 'home extensions' may seem overdone, but if you could add another room to the ground floor or adapt a loft to make a bedroom, this might be better than a move to a bigger house or flat. Just don't arrange major building work to coincide with the later stages of pregnancy!

One couple solved the problem of lack of space by building an extension to their tiny kitchen. This meant that instead of having meals in the living room they were able to eat in comfort in the enlarged kitchen, and in fact they found themselves spending most of their time at home in this comfortable kitchen. This freed the living room for use as their bed-sitter, and their former bedroom for the baby. They got rid of their old bed in favour of a futon, so that the living area was adequate for visitors. 'If the Japanese can live like that, why not us?' they ask. All this did cost a fair amount of money; but they liked it where they lived and were quite sure that a move would have been much more costly.

Money, living conditions, a real sharing of responsibility – all questions to think about. But your health is important too. We'll go on to discuss that now.

CHAPTER 6

HEALTHY MOTHER, HEALTHY CHILD
ARE YOU FIT FOR A BABY?

Reaching her thirtieth birthday can pose a big question for a woman who has put off the decision about having a child while she still felt she had plenty of time. It's a bit daunting, if you do become pregnant, to find yourself described as an 'elderly primagravida'. 'Elderly' in your early thirties? Are you really past it?

Ten or more years ago doctors did believe that there were quite serious risks involved in pregnancy and childbirth once a woman was out of her twenties. Since then, though, so many women have had their first babies perfectly happily at thirty or more – we've looked at some of the reasons for this earlier in this book – that opinions are changing. It's a big generalisation at a time of unemployment and lowered standards of living, but women today are mostly a lot healthier than earlier generations – perhaps because they were born and brought up in the 1950s and 1960s, when the economy wasn't so depressed. There is greater fitness-consciousness, too, and more women than before are taking regular exercise. All this means that today's women stay younger longer, and it follows that they're readier for the physical challenge of childbirth and motherhood in their thirties than their mothers might have been.

That's the positive side of waiting to make the decision. There are some negative aspects, though. Firstly, it seems certain that fertility does decline – gradually, it's true – from the mid-twenties onwards. So it may be more difficult to conceive. Secondly, the risk of the baby being affected by a chromosomal abnormality increases with maternal age. It's normal practice for women over thirty-five to be tested early in pregnancy for foetal abnormality, and to be offered a termination if the baby is found to be affected. Some women reject the idea of abortion even if the baby is abnormal cells. This procedure (amniocentesis) does in having the tests. The first test simply involves taking a blood sample. But if the result of this test indicates that the baby may be affected, some fluid is drawn off from the 'water' surrounding the baby in the womb and this is analysed for the presence of abnormal cells. This procedure (amnio-centesis) does involve a very small risk of miscarriage (1 per cent). So if you're totally opposed to abortion, and therefore wouldn't want a termination in any circumstances, don't have the tests. Still in its early stages in both Britain and the US is another technique – 'chorion villus sampling' – which has the advantage that it can be done much earlier than amniocentesis, so that if abortion is the option it can be performed within the first three months of pregnancy. This method, however, may also involve risk to the foetus (2–4 per cent miscarry) and is so far not available everywhere.

INHERITED
DISABILITIES

Women who are sufferers from, or possible carriers of, some hereditary disability are divided in their perception of 'reproductive technology'. There are many who, for various reasons, feel that they should either not become pregnant, or if they do, should make use of the various techniques available to them to check on the likelihood of a baby suffering from the same disability, including genetic counselling, which can be arranged through a GP.

Antonia spends most of her time in a wheelchair. A spina bifida sufferer, she has nevertheless overcome her mobility problems to enable her to work as a secretary in a multinational company.

'I manage very well, both at work and at home. But in many ways I'm dependent on the help and goodwill of my fellow-workers and on the great amount of domestic jobs my husband does in addition to his rather demanding job as a teacher. Although spina bifida is not a hereditary disability, it does run in families – and unfortunately there were some spina bifida babies in both my and my husband's families, so the likelihood of a baby of ours having spina bifida is probably quite high. We're not willing to run that risk. I couldn't bring myself to have an abortion.

'I've been lucky, since apart from the fact that I can't walk I've had few other problems. What I can't contemplate is having a child who might be worse affected than I am. Also, who could guarantee that he or she would get the sort of support I've had? How would my husband cope with two disabled people? We would have liked a child, of course; but I don't think it would be fair either to the child, or to the people who would eventually have to care for him or her, to have a baby just to satisfy our own desires.'

In complete contrast is the attitude of Micheline Mason, whose disability – osteogenesis imperfecta (brittle bones) – has been inherited by her daughter.

'I always knew that there was a 50 per cent chance that any baby I had would inherit the disability. In my late teens and twenties when I realised this I was quite sure that I should never have a baby. But then I asked myself "Why am I saying that?" It was all to do with my own feelings. Was I saying *I* should never have been born?

'What I had been feeling was mainly fear for myself. I'm single, I am quite severely disabled, I'm only three feet tall. I never made the conscious decision to get pregnant – I didn't know if I could do it. When it happened I decided to go ahead. Everybody – the GP and the hospital consultant – panicked. But I was quite sure that I wouldn't have an abortion and they had to go along with that. At six to seven months a scan showed that the baby was lying in a transverse position and we knew that she, too, had brittle bones. So of course they did a Caesarean with an epidural anaesthetic – because the most dangerous time for the baby with brittle bones is actually being born.

'At two Lucy is crawling, and we spend a lot of time on the floor together. All the furniture is low, so it's the right environment for her. I did take longer to get over the birth than I expected, but I'd organised a whole fleet of people to help me. I've had to learn how to ask for help. The thing is not to look upon yourself as a burden – the people who come along and give me the help I need are nice people – men as well as women – who have no children of their own and really enjoy looking after Lucy. I have a home help twice a week, too.'

Micheline thinks it's important not to *ask permission* from medical or other authority to have a baby. 'Avoid at all costs the sort of person who makes a judgment on your behalf,' she advises. 'Any group can be seen as expendable – on grounds of disability, race or a different culture. It's up to you, not the state or the doctor, to decide what is right for *you*.'

Micheline belongs to the Liberation Network of People with Disabilities. A newsletter keeps members in touch with what's going on, there's a contact list, and, for those who can get to it, an annual meeting.

There are a few other hereditary diseases that families at risk are usually aware of – cystic fibrosis, sickle cell anaemia, haemophilia and Huntingdon's Chorea are some of them. The chances of a baby being affected can be assessed. If the disease is gender-linked and is likely to develop only in boys, for instance, a pregnant woman may wish to be tested through amniocentesis to discover the sex of the baby and, if it's a boy, consider termination. If it's a girl, she will know that the child will be unaffected – but that of course she may be creating a legacy for future generations, since her daughter might have sons. Some will be content to let the future look after itself – because of course it's always possible that at some time treatments will be developed for some sorts of disorder that have hitherto proved intractable. If you're in any doubt about hereditary disorders, and you feel that it's possible that a child might inherit them, you can ask your GP to refer you for genetic counselling. If, like Micheline, you believe that every child has the right to life, and that you are fully prepared for the possible consequences of a pregnancy, it's your right to make the decision, and you will decide to get pregnant, or to continue with any pregnancy that has started.

At this point it should be mentioned that there are some women who do believe that the individual has the right to choose abortion, but who are opposed to the kind of technology referred to above. They see it as not only a manifestation of male power, but as something which may *remove* a woman's right to choose. Like Micheline, they believe that reproductive technology can be carried to the extreme where women who are not 'perfect' may not be *allowed* to bear children. This has sinister links with the eugenics movements of the past, which still exist today, and, even worse, the racial policies of Nazi Germany. These ideas were voiced at a Women's Reproductive Rights conference in 1986 by a group of radical feminists, part of whose statement reads:

'Reproductive technology . . . involves experimentation on embryos for the development of genetic engineering. The focus in research into genetic engineering is on the elimination of "defects." The very concept of "defect" in our society can mean that anyone not considered desirable by the state or medical profession can, through genetic engineering, be manipulated or eliminated from the population. This can translate into sex, race or class (etc) selective breeding.'

Further points from this statement are quoted in the chapter on infertility (see page 129).

HOW FIT ARE YOU?

Another point to consider is your own health. There are some diseases which may be worsened by the strain of pregnancy. If you suffer from multiple sclerosis, for instance, by the time you're in your early thirties you may recently have had the diagnosis, and you should consult the neurologist or other doctor who gave you the diagnosis to get expert opinion on the risks of pregnancy in your case. Some doctors believe that the MS sufferer will experience a flare-up of symptoms during pregnancy and in the months following the birth, but that when the body has 'settled down' again the disease may go into remission. If the prognosis for your particular case is not good you may want to consider the possible long-term problems involved in caring for a baby or an active child. It's a terribly difficult decision.

There may be problems for the diabetic mother, too, but unlike MS, diabetes is a well-understood disease and with the special care offered to the pregnant diabetic, the outcome can be good. Other problems, such as high blood pressure, may also cause difficulties in pregnancy, and if you're in any doubt about *any* health hazard, it's wise to consult a trusted doctor or the appropriate organisation before deciding to have a baby.

Some less serious conditions, such as varicose veins, can be worsened in pregnancy unless precautions are taken to deal with them. Varicose veins often run in families, so if your mother suffered from them it's possible that you will, too. If there's the slightest sign of their developing, get advice and if you become pregnant, wear the appropriate support and take plenty of rest with your feet up. Another problem that may be affected by pregnancy is a 'leaky bladder'. This can be cured by the appropriate 'pelvic floor' exercises – when you've had a baby you should be shown how to do them. Make sure you ask the physiotherapist or midwife.

The final point to make about an 'elderly' woman contemplating pregnancy is one we've touched on throughout this book. It's fatigue. Pregnancy in the later stages *is* tiring, and at any age you'll need as much rest as you can get. And in the first few months of a baby's life most parents find that tiredness or actual exhaustion is their major reaction. No doubt about it, the older you are the less able you are to withstand broken nights and pressurised days without a lot of strain. Everything will settle down after those first months, but to a desperately tired person they can seem endless.

WHAT ABOUT AIDS?

When AIDS (Acquired Immune Deficiency Syndrome) was first identified as a separate disease, its existence and spread were blamed on the male gay population. It soon became clear, however, that it was not confined to homosexuals – some heterosexual women, children and haemophiliacs who had received infected blood, as well as some drugs users, were also affected. Tests have been developed which can identify the presence of AIDS antibodies – meaning that the virus has been present in the body at some time and has caused the body to react to it. At the time of writing, the full implications of a 'positive' HIV test result were not clear, nor was what the risk of an antibody carrier infecting another person is. At first, there was an estimated less than one in ten chance of developing AIDS if the result of the test was positive. A negative result meant that antibodies to the virus had not been detected, but there have been a few cases of the virus being grown from blood that was antibody negative, because it is now known that it can take longer than originally thought for antibodies to appear.

Research is continuing and of course it is hoped

that not only will more reliable tests be developed but that some form of immunisation and/or treatment will be discovered. Anyone who is worried that she may have been infected (and this, it must be emphasised, applies so far to only a tiny minority of women) can ask for the test at a Sexually Transmitted Diseases (STD) clinic before becoming pregnant. The situation on AIDS is changing almost from week to week. Up-to-date information about AIDS as it could affect women – particularly those thinking of AID (artificial insemination by donor) – can be obtained from the Women's Reproductive Rights Information Centre or the Terrence Higgins Trust. If artificial insemination is something that may concern you, see pages 132–5, 180.

POST-NATAL DEPRESSION

One situation you may not have considered seriously is the possibility that you'll be severely depressed after the birth of your baby. We looked briefly at this possibility in chapter 1, as it applied to someone who has already had episodes of depression. But there are women who, for reasons neither they nor their doctors can really explain, are suddenly hit by something much more severe and crippling than the so-called 'normal' baby blues.

Doctors are often not aware that this is happening to a patient. A characteristic of depression, post-natal or otherwise, is that the sufferer feels totally unable to summon up the will or the energy to take any action against it. In the case of a woman who has just had a baby, taking action is even more difficult. For some weeks or months she's a virtual prisoner in her home. She just can't get out or spare the time to go to the doctor's surgery, so, unless her partner or friends or relatives are alerted to her condition, it may go unnoticed by possible sources of help. This is where an aware and sympathetic health visitor can be particularly valuable. She's someone that any mother who feels exhausted, weepy and generally 'down' ought to be able to turn to. The health visitor may take action, or put the woman in touch with a local support group such as those available in many parts of the UK run under the auspices of the National Childbirth Trust or MAMA (the Meet-a-Mum Association).

A depressed woman is often full of guilt. She 'ought' to be on top of the world, delighted with her new baby and happy at the fulfilment of her dreams. She feels very bad about her reaction, so it's quite useless and damaging for a family member to point out to her how lucky she is, and how ungrateful for her good fortune; and as with any depressed person, the exhortation to 'pull yourself together' is just as hurtful. No one wishes more desperately that she could than the sufferer herself.

If you should find yourself in this situation – and of course it's not nearly as common as some people believe – the main thing to remember is that you should make your feelings clear to someone who will take them seriously and get help. Don't behave as though it's all your fault: how do we know that a combination of hormonal changes plus the fatigue of pregnancy, childbirth and the constant care of a new baby aren't causing this condition, and shouldn't we accept this possibility, rather than blaming personal weakness?

On page 28 the survey carried out by researchers at London's Thomas Coram Foundation was mentioned. The team did find that during the first six months of the babies' lives some women had become depressed, worried and over-stressed. But out of the ninety women in the group, only three had had medical treatment for depression: and two-thirds thought that their present life was 'ideal' or said that they were 'very satisfied' – a high rating on any job-satisfaction scale.

In this book we have looked at some of the more negative aspects of parenthood, though there have been some hints at possible solutions to the problems too. Earlier the point was made that awareness of potential difficulties, and action taken to forestall them if possible, always pays off. If all goes well, and problems don't arise, you'll be able to dismiss these 'awful warnings' as unnecessarily alarmist. But if you do meet difficulties, you'll have been prepared for them and possibly know how to take evasive action, before real depression sets in. Not everyone takes parenthood in her stride, but undertaken with some of the cons as well as the pros firmly in mind, it's much more likely to be a happy experience for mother and child.

FIT FOR A BABY

In recent years a new worry for prospective parents has come on to the scene. It's 'pre-conceptual planning'. Books have been written, conferences held and organisations set up to encourage mothers and fathers to reach a peak of fitness well before attempting to conceive. Obviously, the healthier both parents are before the woman becomes pregnant, the better able they are to take the strains both before and after the birth, and the more likely it is that both baby and parents will benefit. It's certainly a good idea to eat sensibly, take adequate exercise and rest, and avoid stress – and if getting into good shape to have the baby results in building up healthy habits, that's a lasting bonus. Pre-pregnancy is the time to make strenuous efforts to stop smoking – which everyone now accepts may be a serious health hazard for women and men at any time, but which can also affect the unborn baby. There's some evidence that fathers as well as mothers should stop smoking before conception takes place, and very strong evidence that babies living in an environment filled with cigarette smoke are more likely to suffer from respiratory problems than those in non-smoking households. Similarly, it's a good idea for both parents to cut down on alcohol in the pre-conceptual period, especially as during pregnancy a woman would be well advised to cut it out altogether.

These are common-sense steps which it may be a lot easier to take in the months before pregnancy rather than leaving them to the time when conception has actually taken place – thus avoiding both the difficulties of adopting new life-styles all at once, as well as the possible hazards to the unborn child. The danger of becoming too obsessed by 'pre-conceptual care' ideas is, of course, that the woman who didn't intend to get pregnant, and therefore hasn't done much to improve her health or stop smoking or drinking, can be upset and feel guilty that she may have damaged her child. Like all good ideas and advances in self-care, this idea – that preparing for pregnancy is important – can be carried to excess, and can join the other well-known guilt-producers for women; the 'failure' to manage childbirth without analgesics, the 'failure' to breast-feed, the 'failure' to enjoy twenty four hour-a-day involvement with one's child.

Readers of this book, however, are likely to have some time to prepare for pregnancy, and without becoming over concerned, can see that they take steps to adopt healthy ways of living. There's nothing outlandish about the pre-pregnancy regime – it's simply adopting the guidelines publicised by the Health Education Authority in Britain and similar bodies elsewhere. Simply put, it involves adopting a healthy diet and taking a reasonable amount of exercise.

A healthy diet means one in which all fats are cut to about 30 per cent of calories consumed (the British average is around 40 per cent), and most of the cutting-down should involve fats of animal origin. An easy way to achieve this reduction is to use skimmed or semi-skimmed milk, low-fat cheese, use less butter, and to eat less red meat. Sugar in its various forms is something else to avoid – you can very quickly become used to sugarless tea and coffee – and by looking at the labels of prepared foods you can avoid those in which sugar appears high on the list of ingredients. Salt, too, is frequently used to excess – if a very little is added in cooking it should be possible to banish salt from the table.

These are the *don'ts*. The *dos* don't involve anything you could possibly see as a sacrifice. *Do* eat fish instead of meat, plenty of fresh fruit and vegetables, peas, beans of all kinds, lentils, nuts, sesame seeds, oats in various forms, wholemeal bread and wholemeal flour. Cook by baking, boiling or steaming, but eat an uncooked meal once a day. Angela Phillips' book *Your Body, Your Baby, Your Life* (1983) has some useful suggestions for pregnant women who find difficulty in catering for themselves *and* their families.

The question of vitamin and mineral supplementation is more controversial. On the whole the medical profession believes that with a good, healthy diet, supplements are unnecessary. On the other hand, there are those who believe that anyone living largely on processed foods, or who hasn't access to really fresh vegetables, will lack certain vitamins and something like a multi-vitamin pill a day may be helpful. The issue is particularly confusing because different countries have different 'minimum daily requirements' of vitamins regarded as necessary to maintain health. On the whole the minimum recommended intakes of vitamins and minerals in Britain are lower than those recommended in the United States. A good baby book will give guidelines for pregnant women – see pages 175–6. In the pre-pregnancy period the amounts are the same.

If you do decide to take supplements, it's important to remember that it's possible to overdose, particularly with the fat-soluble vitamins A,D and E. Study the labels and, if you're taking more than one tablet or capsule, remember that you might be taking more than the recommended amount, and adjust accordingly.

When you are pregnant you can expect that any necessary supplements will be prescribed for you by your clinic doctor or GP.

Something that may concern a woman in the pre-conceptual period is the question of additives. Most processed foods now contain 'permitted' additives with their 'E' numbers. These aren't much help unless you have access to a book that explains what they are and what their possible side-effects might be. For a useful book on the subject, see page 175.

The amount of exercise you take depends very largely on your existing habits. If you play tennis, jog or swim, attend an exercise class or play any kind of active sport, you'll already be in good shape. Obviously when you're thinking of having a baby you'll want to maintain your usual forms of exercise. How far you continue them into pregnancy must be a matter for consultation at your ante-natal check-ups. But if you're not already taking regular exercise, it really is a good idea, well before becoming pregnant, to start taking longish, brisk walks every day. If you're really out of condition, start by walking briskly for ten minutes, then slowing down completing a full half-hour. After a few days, walk briskly for fifteen minutes out of the half-hour, and so on until the whole time is spent walking briskly. Do this twice a day, and if you hate taking exercise just for the sake of it, do this brisk walking part of the way to work and back, or to the shops or on some other errand. This kind of exercise relieves stress, improves heart and lung function and makes you feel generally much more lively. And it's good training for childbirth. If disability means that daily walks are impossible, ask your health visitor or physiotherapist to show you exercises tailored to your particular needs.

DRUGS AND IMMUNISATIONS

Anyone taking 'recreational' or non-prescribed drugs should kick the habit before becoming pregnant. Since most of these drugs are addictive, you'll almost certainly need help (see page 181). Not so well recognised are the dangers to pregnant women and their babies of very large numbers of prescribed drugs – and these include not only the well-publicised hazards of certain drugs which have been proved to cause birth defects. Anyone reading the small print of advertisements in the medical press for a variety of prescription medicines would be aware that very many of them are 'contra-indicated' in pregnancy. If you intend to become pregnant you should ask the prescribing doctor specifically whether the drug s/he has given you could have undesirable side-effects in pregnancy, and, unless your health is completely dependent on this medication, suggest that you cease to take it.

Another precaution to be taken before you become pregnant is a check on whether or not you are immune to Rubella (German measles). A simple test will establish this, and you can be immunised if necessary. This should be done at least three months before you become pregnant – so if you're even considering having a baby and you're not sure whether you were immunised in your schooldays, you should be checked. If you have to have the immunisation now, use contraception for the next three months.

STOPPING CONTRACEPTION

If you have been using barrier methods of contraception, you can simply stop using them once you have decided to try to become pregnant. Some women get pregnant within a month – others have to wait longer and, in fact, the average time between stopping contraception and conceiving is around six months.

With the Pill, the situation is rather different. Many authorities suggest that there should be no attempt to become pregnant until the Pill has been stopped for six months, others say three. There seems to be a *very small* risk of abnormality in the foetus if conception takes place immediately. Meanwhile, barrier methods should be used. But there's another worry experienced by many Pill-users. A sizeable proportion of women find that they don't re-establish menstruation for quite a while after coming off the Pill, and if they do start to have periods, these are so irregular that it's difficult to estimate the most fertile time of the month. Medical opinion is that if a woman does not menstruate (and ovulate) regularly after two or three months off the Pill, this is because her periods and ovulation were never regular and fully established. She may have gone on to the Pill without realising that this was the case. Thus, it is said, whether or not she was ever on the Pill has made no difference – she would probably be having irregular periods anyway.

Anyone, whether or not she has been on the Pill, who fails to conceive after trying for a year should seek medical advice. For a further discussion of infertility or subfertility see chapter 9.

SEX IN PREGNANCY

Along with all the worries experienced by women who are pregnant or intending to become so – and many of them are *not* self-generated – is the fear that sex with penetration may damage the developing foetus. Can the newly-implanted egg be displaced in some way by vigorous sex; if so, and supposing I may be pregnant, should I avoid intercourse? some women wonder. There is no evidence that this can happen at any stage of a pregnancy unless something is already going wrong. And, if you avoided sex when you *might* be pregnant, and in fact you weren't, your chances of conception at the next time of ovulation would be nil!

Anyone who is concerned about male penetration at any point in her pregnancy may be reassured if she looks at the illustrations in Miriam Stoppard's book *Pregnancy and Birth Book* (1986) (see page 176). The drawings show positions in which you can have sexual intercourse comfortably in the later stages of pregnancy, when your usual position might be uncomfortable. Stoppard also makes the point in her text that there are other ways to have satisfying sex when a woman's bulk can make penetration difficult.

This isn't a 'baby book', so we don't discuss baby care here, or give detailed information about pregnancy and childbirth, but there are plenty of books you can buy or consult, a good Health Education Council large format book that's usually provided free at the ante-natal clinic, and recommended books are listed on page 176.

Before we consider practicalities for those who have made a decision, it's worth looking again at some of the pros and cons already discussed. You might find the next few pages helpful.

CHAPTER 7

PAUSE FOR THOUGHT
ARE YOU READY TO DECIDE?

In the first six chapters of this book we've looked at many of the pros and cons of parenthood, and read what women and men in a variety of circumstances have had to say on the subject. As someone who is still unsure about her own position, you may have been able to identify with some of the ideas and experiences outlined up to this point, while rejecting others. The result may have been enlightenment of a sort – or even greater confusion. If that's how you feel, it's time now to summarise the factors that lead some people to go ahead and have a baby, while others conclude that, for a variety of reasons, they would do better to remain childless.

It's not suggested that the following is a comprehensive checklist – you won't be able to tick off the items and answer 'yes' or 'no' to the points made – but it's offered as a help to those who usually find it useful to balance up the advantages or disadvantages of any possible course of action. Even if you're normally impetuous in making decisions, and prepared to take the consequences if they turn out to be the wrong ones, you might like now to reconsider your position, if only to reject such a formal approach to a very personal matter.

Each section below asks a question and suggests the answers some people might offer. If you agree with most of the 'positive' answers, this may help you to go ahead and try to get pregnant. If most of the answers are less positive, you may be wise to think again.

Why have you considered having a baby?

It's only natural.
I feel like just letting it happen.
I've always assumed I'd have children.
It would fulfil me as a woman.
I feel like testing out my fertility.
I owe it to posterity, to the continuance of the human race.
It shows some faith in the future in these dangerous times.
I love children.
I need someone of my own to love.
I feel very protective and maternal.
It's a gut feeling I can't resist.
It's a more rewarding job than any other.

If most of the above echo your own feelings, you'll probably be ready to make a positive decision.

Does anyone else want you to have a baby?

My partner wants a child.
My parents want grandchildren.
It's part of my culture to have lots of children.
My partner always assumed we'd have children. I can't let him/her down.
Our relationship would be more secure if we had a baby.
All my friends are having babies.
I'm sick of being asked when I'm going to produce.

If you've experienced most of these pressures, you might ask yourself what you really want, and question the right of others to influence you, especially if you believe that, left to you, the decision would be against getting pregnant.

Does anyone not want you to have a baby?

My partner is definitely against having children.
My partner says 'go ahead' and that it's entirely up to me.

My partner says 'go ahead, but don't expect me
   to develop any interest in the baby.'
My partner might leave me if I got pregnant.
I think my partner will change when the baby's
   actually there.
Everyone says I'm too old to have a baby.
My doctor says I'm too disabled to risk
   pregnancy.
My friends say I'd be mad to give up my career
   to have a baby.
My friends say I've no idea how difficult it is to
   bring up a child.
Everyone says it's irresponsible to have a child
   as a single parent.
My employer/colleagues would be severely
   inconvenienced if I left work.
My parents think I'm too immature to be a
   mother.
I don't want to conform to the appalling
   stereotype that black/poor women are
   irresponsible when they have children.
My partner and I have different religions – our
   churches don't approve of marriages like
   ours.
Straight society disapproves of lesbian mothers –
   our child could have a bad time.

*Here, too, consult your own feelings. By all means consider
the objections others raise (some might be valid) but
question, too, the motives behind them. You may still be
prepared to go it alone, or to change some aspect of your life
which would make it possible to have the baby you really
want.*

**Could you
adapt?**

I know we'd have to make many changes in the
   way we live.
I understand that I'd be unable to come and go
   and do things on impulse as I do now.
People make too much fuss about babies. If I

handled things right, the baby would adapt
to me, not me to her.

If you organise things properly, a baby doesn't
have to take over your whole life.

I believe in muddling through.

I'm the sort of person who gets absorbed in
anything I've decided to do.

It's only for a few years – I can spare that out of
my life.

*Much of this book is devoted to making the point that
having a baby does change your life. For a majority, it's
undoubtedly a change for the better; for some, the reverse.
You just need to be sure that you see this change as positive,
not as making painful sacrifices.*

What about your health?

I'm young and strong and I stand up well to
strain.

Childbirth terrifies me – I'm a coward when it
comes to physical pain.

I'm easily tired; I wonder how I'd manage with
too little sleep.

I know the first few weeks may be exhausting –
but they pass.

I may be lucky and have an undemanding
baby.

I am disabled – I wonder if I could cope.

I am disabled – would it be fair to the child?

I am disabled, but I wouldn't hesitate to ask for
help from others.

There's an hereditary disease in my family, but
I'd still run the risk of my baby inheriting it.

If it was found that my baby was suffering from
a disability, I would have an abortion.

I'm worried about my ability to breast-feed.

If breast-feeding proved too difficult, I'd be
quite ready to bottle-feed.

Motherhood is too important to me to be
dissuaded from it on grounds of health.

Pregnancy, childbirth and child care are all stressful in different ways. If there are real risks to your health or that of a child, take the best advice you can, but still make up your own mind.

Would the timing be right?

Once we've decided to have a baby, we might as well get on with it.

The time will never be ideal, but I can't wait forever.

I'm over thirty, if I don't have a baby soon I never will.

Just because I'm in my thirties that's no reason to be panicked into pregnancy.

I'm not sure enough of my relationship to get pregnant at present.

If I waited a few more years I'd have a better job to go back to.

If I waited a few more years, we'd have more money and security.

I don't think it's right to have a baby in living conditions such as ours.

I'm not mature enough to have a baby.

My job is a dead-end. I'll never get anywhere in it, so having a baby now is a better option.

Bringing up children is more important than any other job. I want several, so I'll have to get pregnant soon.

I think I may have a fertility problem. The sooner I know, the sooner I'll get treatment.

Of course your answers to this question depend on individual situations and feelings. The second item above sums up many women's attitude – but if you're in real doubt, can you wait?

If you plan to stay at home, could you cope with isolation?

I have plenty of friends with children – we'd see a lot of each other.

I'm a self-contained person – I don't fear loneliness.

I worry because all my friends and neighbours go out to work.

If I got desperate, I'd overcome shyness and approach other mothers.

I've already tried making local friends, but there's no one I can relate to.

I'd contact a mother-and-baby group, or start one myself.

I know that I'd get depressed, being shut away from adult company.

Looking after a baby is a full-time job, so I wouldn't have time to feel lonely.

I think I might become a bore to my partner and myself.

I need stimulation – I wonder if a baby would provide enough?

Housework is hateful and that's what I'd be spending so much time doing.

Your response to this question depends partly on your own personality and partly on your particular circumstances. As ever, good back-up and the possibility of continuing contact with the outside world would be sanity-savers. If you foresee depression – and it's a recognised problem of housebound mothers – you'll have to consider whether you could change yourself or your circumstances.

Would you make a 'good enough' parent?

I don't know anything about child psychology or child development.

I've never had anything to do with babies.

I see my friends' mistakes: would I do any better?

The main requirement seems to be patience, and I've got that.

I'm so easily bored.

I think I could cope with a baby, but I'd be
   hopeless with a difficult adolescent.
I don't care for babies, but I'd enjoy an older
   child.
I'm an anxious person; I'd find the
   responsibility terrifying.
I think I might get over-involved.
I think I might be over-protective.
I'm untidy and disorganised by nature – I can't
   manage my own life, so how would I be with
   another's?
I hate routine, but children seem to need it.
I'm willing to give up everything to have a
   child.
I'd try to maintain my independence, and see
   motherhood as just part of my life.
I'd try to bring up a child to have a mind of her
   own, but I'm very unsure about the amount
   of direction that needs.

If you agree with most of the above, you share your sense of insecurity with a majority of women. Ask yourself how important to YOU each item is. Could you overcome anxieties and uncertainties, or are they so real that they could make motherhood hazardous for you or the child? Or would you learn by doing – as you have other jobs?

Perhaps few of the answers here have agreed with your particular feelings or identified your particular dilemma. Although Part Two is actually intended to offer suggestions to those who have already made up their minds one way or the other, reading it might still clarify matters for you.

PART TWO

CHAPTER 8

DOWN TO EARTH
CAN YOU PLAN AHEAD?

If after reading so far, you've decided to go ahead, this chapter is for you. But if you're still unsure – largely on the grounds that you're not quite certain how much of the essential back-up we've discussed earlier you're likely to get – this chapter could help you focus on the possible problems. So, bearing in mind that it is primarily aimed at those who've decided to become pregnant, it might be a good idea not to skip it; reading it could help in the decision process.

ANTE-NATAL CARE

Ante-natal clinics in Britain have acquired a bad name – not because they fail to offer useful help and advice and monitor conscientiously the health of mother and baby, but because of the sometimes inhumane conditions, poor organisation and long waiting and travelling times attending them often involve. These strictures apply principally to some hospital-based clinics. Where ante-natal care is solely or largely given by individual doctors or midwives in the more familiar environment of the health centre or surgery, most women are a lot happier.

Local circumstances vary, but whatever system applies in your district, you're strongly advised to take advantage of the ante-natal care offered. Yes, there may be interminable waits; yes, every time you go you'll see a different doctor; yes, it may seem a waste of time to attend a clinic for a two-minute blood test and a one-minute consultation. But where pregnant women do take advantage of what's on offer, there's a much greater chance of problems being identified and treated, and a satisfactory outcome to the pregnancy, than there would be if these routine appointments were missed. This doesn't mean you should accept poor conditions and impersonal handling without protest. If a group of women who feel they've cause for complaint *do* complain, there's strength in numbers, and notice is more likely to be taken. If you don't get anywhere, one of the organisations listed on page 179 may offer advice and help.

Most good baby books explain the usual procedure at the ante-natal clinic – some recommended books are listed on pages 175–6, and once you're at the clinic you'll probably be given some literature, including, in Britain, a very helpful Health Education Council *Pregnancy Book* (first published in 1984).

One thing that worries many pregnant women, however, is the effect that some of the tests offered – particularly the ante-natal ultrasound screening test – might have on the unborn baby. British obstetricians, on the whole, claim that the benefits of this test far outweigh what they claim to be unproven risks. Organisations representing women concerned about the maternity services, however, have produced what they regard as firm evidence of some hazards. In these circumstances it's hard to offer firm advice – undoubtedly ultrasound can detect some abnormalities or development problems, so its value can't be dismissed out of hand. Perhaps the best, if tentative, suggestion is that anyone who is anxious about possible ill-effects of routine screening might consider having one ultrasound examination, and if all is found to be normal, avoid having any routine tests offered later.

Blood and other tests offered aren't likely to cause any problems. If, however, a blood test shows that the baby may be affected by an abnormality such as spina bifida, for the woman who would consider a termination of pregnancy if her baby were shown to be abnormal, there is a dilemma. The next stage is the test known as amniocentesis, and this does carry a small (about 1 per cent) risk of miscarriage. This test can also show whether the baby has Down's syndrome, and is usually offered only to women over thirty five if this, rather than 'neural tube defect', is possible. Suppose the baby is, in fact, normal? This is a tiny risk that some women are prepared to take. But, as we've seen earlier (page 87), if there are no circumstances in which you would wish to have a termination, you can decide not to have this test.

BACK-UP IN PREGNANCY

Since you've already discussed all the pros and cons of having a baby and will have decided (reinforced by this book and the book *Going Solo* by Jean Renvoize) that you'll need full support from partner, house sharers, friends and relatives if you're to manage successfully, it's not too early to put this into practice. Some women feel off-colour or faint and experience pregnancy sickness as actually the first signs that they're pregnant. You're not an invalid when you're pregnant, but you do need some help from other concerned adults. Even if you don't experience these 'symptoms', as pregnancy advances you'll need more rest, help with carrying heavy shopping, and so on, and someone to take over some of the household jobs you normally do. If your partner or other adult(s) with whom you're living can't do simple cooking, cleaning, laundry and other such jobs, it's high time s/he learnt. Part of the decision you've made about having a baby has depended on an agreement to share – not only baby care but the myriad of jobs involved in daily living; so if this isn't already happening, the next few months should see the arrangement working smoothly.

It's also very comforting to experience the support of another adult on your ante-natal check-up visits, and certainly at any birth preparation classes you attend. If no partner is available, the next best is a good friend. Conventionally, many mothers accompany their pregnant daughters to the clinic, so there's absolutely no reason why a friend should feel excluded, and she can be helpful in reminding you of questions you wanted to ask, and making a note of any advice you're offered to reinforce your memory. Most clinics accept this: if you meet refusal, protest.

Partners or friends who attend ante-natal clinics and classes are receiving birth preparation, as well as you, and will be all the readier to join you at the actual birth, and better briefed as to their own role as supporters. They'll have joined you in the decision whether to have a hospital or home birth (where this is possible) and support you in this decision. (For a discussion on home versus hospital births see the books listed on pages 175–6.)

WORKING IN PREGNANCY

Long gone are the days when pregnant women were treated as fragile creatures (if they were of the middle class) or primitive beasts of burden able to give birth in a field and continue their heavy labour within a couple of hours. In theory, at least, modern social security systems provide time off work both before and after childbirth, and in Britain, as in some other countries, job security for the majority should they wish to return to work after maternity leave. If in doubt about your position, look at the Appendix (page 169) and perhaps sound out your employers.

Most women will plan to remain at work as long as possible before their baby's birth, and in general this seems to be a good idea. The middle months of pregnancy are often the time when a woman feels at her best – provided she gets adequate rest, she's energetic but relaxed, and perfectly well able to continue in her job. Unfortunately for some, though, the first few weeks of pregnancy are a great trial – morning or, more often, evening sickness, and nausea during the day can sap energy and make work difficult. Since this situation is almost invariably of short duration, it would be a pity to give up work at this stage, only to find in a few weeks' time that everything had settled down and you felt perfectly well able to cope with the normal demands of your working life.

If you do experience pregnancy sickness, it's at this early stage that your partner or friend can be very helpful. Many women find that a cup of tea in bed, and possibly a piece of dry toast, dispels nausea first thing in the morning. If evening nausea is the problem, and cooking makes you feel even worse, a light meal set before you for which you have had no responsibility can do the trick. Since most authorities suggest that 'little and often' is the way to eat in this situation, you could find it helpful to have a supply of plain yogurt at the ready. At this stage, too, you could hand over shopping – some perfectly healthy women feel faint if they have to stand for any length of time at the check-out, and this, too, is a passing phase. If you're working, try to avoid rush-hour travel by renegotiating working hours for a few weeks.

Although very many women in sedentary and light work are well able to continue their jobs until late in their pregnancy, some research carried out in France a few years ago shows that women in physically exhausting jobs such as cleaners, social workers and shop workers tend to have a higher incidence of premature babies. The worst outlook, so the research found, was for women whose jobs involved a lot of standing in hot conditions. Standing for any length of time affects the circulation, and this can mean a restriction of the baby's growth.

Women working with X-rays, certain chemicals, or who are exposed to above-average sources of infection would probably be wise to consider changing jobs, working shorter hours or stopping work sooner rather than later.

Although government and industry deny that there are any hazards connected with the use of VDUs (visual display units), there's a widespread belief that the incidence of miscarriage among users is significantly high. In Britain the trade unions concerned advise women to ask to be transferred to other work when they are pregnant and most employers are willing to agree to this. If you work with VDUs and you meet resistance to the idea of transfer, you should take the matter up with your trade union or association.

If the above suggestions are rather disquieting, you can take comfort from the fact that the French survey showed that women who continue working in pregnancy are less likely to have premature babies than are housewives. With the exceptions mentioned earlier, it's far safer to go on working up to within ten or eleven weeks of the birth than to smoke cigarettes, drink alcohol regularly and eat an inadequate diet.

WHEN TO STOP

For most women, then, the main factor affecting their decision about continuing to work will be the financial one. Obviously the longer you can work the more money you can put towards the cost of equipping the baby or saving for the future. In general, the average time of stopping work (about ten weeks before the birth) is about right. It's at that point that you may feel heavy and unwieldy, tiring easily and really ready to take things a bit more quietly in preparation for the efforts ahead. But if you work at home, or have an enjoyable and not-too-demanding job that doesn't involve difficult journeys to and from work, you may feel it's worth carrying on almost until the last moment, and saving some of your 'leave' until the end of the post-natal maternity leave period, which will give you longer to settle your baby down and find substitute care for when you do return to work.

On pages 169–73 you will find information about the legislation affecting pregnant women and working mothers – grants and allowances, maternity leave, job security, etc.

WHO'S TO CARE?

A very important factor in your decision to go ahead and try to become pregnant must be the way you plan to live after the baby is born. If you're a single woman or your partner is away from home a great deal you'll have been wise to plan just how you're going to get the back-up help you'll often need, even if you don't plan to go out to work. Clearly if you're going to continue to work outside the home some really watertight plans should be in the making well before you need to put them into effect.

As we've seen earlier in this book, some couples are able to reverse roles wholly or partially, job-share, work at home or in some other way ensure that their children are cared for by one or other parent at different times of the day or week. This is a trend that's slowly gaining ground – but it has to be said that professional people and those in jobs where freelancing or a home-based business are possible find the idea a lot easier to implement. For the majority, it's still the man who's the major money-earner, and sheer economics dictates that he'll be the one who spends more of his time out of the home than the less well-paid woman. This might sound like a neat solution to the problem of child care – but of course it isn't. A man may have more earning power – but what if he's unemployed; what if his 'higher' pay is still very low? In these circumstances huge numbers of women have been forced back to work part- or full-time. And that's not to mention the many hundreds of thousands who enjoy their work, enjoy working with others, enjoy the feeling of freedom and independence that having a job outside the home can bring. They know that building up job experience and earning their own money is the best possible insurance in an uncertain future. They don't want to repeat the experience of an older generation, when women were economically powerless to leave a bad marriage or felt useless and bereft of purpose once their children had grown up.

You may decide, as many do, that if it's financially possible you'll wait until your children reach school age before you'll think of working outside the home. There's a lot to be said for this – provided you don't find yourself shut in, literally and metaphorically, day in and day out with your child alone. Once more it comes to a question of back-up – if you have a partner who doesn't work long hours, friends in the same position as yourself, or family members you can call on in an emergency or to give you a break, you may find these few years very enjoyable and rewarding.

It's probable though, that as a reader of this book you may be the sort of woman who will not wish to devote 100 per cent of her time to her baby, once she's past the early months. It's not always possible to plan everything down to a T before you're actually in the situation of having the baby, but in the months left to you before that happens, it would be very wise to have some idea of the possibilities open to you for having your baby looked after while you're at work. We'll assume that you aren't able to call upon your partner for more than a share of the care at evenings, weekends and holidays and in emergencies. You'll expect him or her to participate fully at those times, of course – it was that possibility that weighted the balance when you decided to go ahead and try to get pregnant. But because both of you will be working, both of you will need some form of regular care for your baby or toddler, and the responsibility for deciding what kind you want, and arranging it, should be shared too. It isn't just your job, as the mother, to organise all this – your partner should be quite as involved as you.

SUPPORT
SYSTEM

Let's look at some of the sources of help with the children (and perhaps with the home, too). First of all, you might have to decide whether your job after the birth is to be full- or part-time. What would suit someone working nine to five every weekday would be unnecessary for a mother working half-days.

Local authorities' day nurseries are intended for

working mothers – but because of lack of resources their availability is very uneven and, in any case, they usually have places only for the children of single mothers or those living in very deprived or unsuitable circumstances. There are a few workplace nurseries – you'll know if your employer provides one. They're often quite expensive and recent legislation in Britain may force parents to pay tax on any 'perk' of this kind subsidised by their employers. There are private nurseries, too, and these can be even more expensive. Unless you're very well paid, child care could swallow up such a huge proportion of your earnings that you'd be almost out of pocket by working. If you're career-building, you may be willing to pay this price, but if money is your main object, you might have to think again about using a private nursery.

Most working parents whose income isn't substantial opt for child-minders. In Britain, anyone regularly taking a child into her home for payment should be registered with the local authority social service department, which holds the names of approved child-minders. Arrangements about hours, rates of pay and other matters are made direct with the minder. Registration with the local authority should ensure that the minder's home is adequate from the health and safety point of view, and the number of children the minder is allowed to take is also regulated. However, registration is no guarantee that the minder and you, as the baby's parent, will see eye-to-eye on every aspect of the care of your child, so it's very important to talk to her and get some idea of her attitudes towards 'discipline', exercise, rest and play, and whether she's the sort of person who will help your child develop as you hope or whether she's more passive and less communicative than you'd like.

If you've got the room, and you can afford it, you may consider employing a mother's help (who will do some housework and take limited charge of your child) or an au pair. Neither is suitable for full-time, sole care of a young child, though they might be useful as part-time minders for older children or if you are working at home. An au pair, according to government regulations, may work only five hours a day, and must be given time off for language study.

A solution that suits many parents is a local 'granny'. She's usually a middle-aged or older woman who has had children of her own, enjoys looking after young children and, with no pressing home ties, can be flexible about her hours. She may be glad to do a little housework as well as look after the baby. Often a very rewarding relationship can be developed with a proxy granny of this kind, and she'll remain to look after your older children after school hours and in the holidays when she's no longer needed full-time for a baby or toddler. A straightforward local advertisement may conjure up this paragon.

The really well-off will consider a living-in qualified NNEB nanny, who can command a salary of not less than £80 per week at 1986 levels. But if you and a friend could afford to share a nanny, with one of you providing the accommodation she'll need, and the same parent or another having the children and nanny during the day, this kind of help will be less expensive. The same applies to employing a shared daily nanny.

This arrangement works well for Sarah and Lynne. They met through attending their doctor's 'well baby' clinic. Each confessed her frustration at not being able to find suitable child care to enable them to return to work as they had hoped. They decided to join forces in an attempt to work out a solution. As Sarah explains:

'What we came up with was a very good solution. Through contacts we found a young woman who had some nannying experience, though she wasn't actually a trained nanny. She didn't want a living-in job, and neither of us wanted someone to live in, either – we didn't have the room. So what we do is this: for half the week I take my toddler to Lynne's house, and the nanny looks after both children there, making lunch and snacks for them, taking them out for walks and to play in the park or the garden. The other half of the week they come to my place. We alternate weeks so that one week Lynne has them for three days and the next they come to me, with the other half of the partnership having the children and the nanny for two days. This means that we really share the expenses, and another bonus is that the two children have regular company and they have a variety of toys. We liaise about toys and make sure they're never duplicated so they have a wider variety than each could have alone. Just at first the children were a bit possessive about "their" toys, but we've got over that. It looks as though we'll be able to keep up this arrangement until the two of them reach school age. At that point we'll try to find someone to do the same sort of child-minding on an after-school and holiday basis.'

A teacher who does have room in her house for someone to live in found an arrangement whereby an older woman looked after the children of three families in return for accommodation, food and a small salary, with weekends, school holidays and a shorter-than-average working day making up for a less-than-average wage. The families concerned shared costs.

But when considering the full cost of employing someone, remember you must also take into account the quite considerable additional cost of her living in, or of one or two meals a day if she comes in daily. In either case, she'll probably be liable for income tax – and you for seeing it's paid – and for National Insurance. Many 'domestic' employees expect their employer to pay both shares of the insurance, so that can be a hefty weekly sum, too. Addresses of agencies are given on pages 179–80.

The Working Mother's Handbook (first published in 1982, see page 176) is particularly strong on information about child care – how to get it, how much it costs, and what your legal liabilities are.

Your own mother or another relative may be glad to take your baby on a regular basis – but don't assume this! Many older women whose own children have grown up and left home are beginning to taste and enjoy freedom from that kind of responsibility for the first time in their lives. Even if you agree to put the arrangement on a business footing, be sure that she isn't once more bowing to the demands of her family and allowing their needs to take priority over her own. She, too, may want to go out to work, get further education or work in a political or voluntary organisation. So tread warily!

If you intend to work part-time, and can find another mother who wants to do the same, provided you can fit in your timing with each other, this can be a cost-free and very satisfactory way of looking after two or more babies or toddlers. If she's already a friend, you'll probably have a lot of ideas in common and so there shouldn't be any clashes between you. When the children are close in age, they'll enjoy the company and benefit from a change of scene without feeling threatened by surroundings that are too alien.

These are some of the options. Think about them now.

We've referred above to the importance of seeing eye-to-eye, as far as possible, with the child-minder or other person who is going to look after your child. But there may be other problems: some mothers are surprised when they're struck by pangs of jealousy. Could it be that their child actually prefers the woman who looks after her each day to the mother who puts her to bed, cares for her at weekends and loves her all the time? The difficulty is less likely to arise when the child is looked after by more than one person – at a playgroup – but even then, as mothers of school-age children know very well, many are adept at playing off one adult (the teacher) against another (the parent).

Although at times it may seem that a mother's fears

are justified, children do know who is really the major carer, because it doesn't depend on the hours spent but on the love and concern that's demonstrated every day in the parent-and-child relationship. If you find that you hate to share your child with another person, it might help to ask yourself whether you aren't being over-possessive – and to take action, if you can, to widen the child's circle of friends; adults and children. Children brought up to accept friendship and affection from friends and relatives and to give them their love and trust can only gain by the experience, and won't, in their turn, be so possessive about their parents. And to organise frequent changes of carer isn't the answer – a child loses in a sense of security and stability far more than her mother gains in keeping other adults at a distance.

As we noted earlier, though, well-laid and apparently workable plans can go wrong – not only because unexpected emergencies are more frequent than you may believe possible, but because it may be that your individual child has a particular problem. Since you've probably already made up your mind to go ahead, this won't deter you. The difficulties quoted by two women referred to in chapter 5 may not be precisely the ones that affect you, but similar ones could. All that you can do now is to be prepared to be flexible: don't meet problems more than halfway, but do accept that the coming change in your life could be even greater than you think.

Yes, plans can go wrong – and sometimes in unexpected and painful ways. What happens if you decide to have a baby – and find you can't? The next chapter discusses this problem.

CHAPTER 9

INFERTILITY, SUBFERTILITY, LOSS
WHAT IF THINGS GO WRONG?

Your decision is made. If you have a regular male partner, you've stopped using barrier methods of contraception, and if you were on the Pill, you stopped taking that at least three months ago. So now it's just a question of waiting for that missed period and the other signs of pregnancy that you expect.

If you have decided to have a baby as a single woman, through sexual intercourse with a chosen man or by AID, for you, too, it's just a question of waiting. Two or three months pass, during which you will have attempted to become pregnant – but whatever your situation, you're not worried, because you know that on average it can take longer than that to conceive. After six months of 'trying' at the right time of the month, you may become more than a little anxious. After a few months more, the worry grows. Is there something wrong with you or the male sperm? If you're in your thirties, have you perhaps left it too late? If you've had an abortion, could that have affected your fertility? Have years on the Pill messed you up in some way? Are you one of the one in eight couples who are infertile, or the unknown percentage of single women who can't conceive?

Most doctors won't consider that there's a problem until a woman has being trying to start a baby for at least a year. If you're in your mid-thirties or older, a sympathetic doctor will suggest a referral for fertility tests sooner than that – provided you convince her or him that you are having intercourse often enough round the menstrual mid-cycle – or indeed having intercourse at all, because (very rarely) couples present who are not having intercourse with penetration, and don't understand that this – or AID – is necessary in order to conceive.

When you're having intercourse several times a week, or you have been making frequent attempts at AID, and still don't conceive, it's very natural to be concerned. Until recently the medical establishment has shown little understanding of the desperation many would-be parents feel when, month after month, their hopes are dashed. Relax, said the doctors – it's because you're all tensed up that you don't get pregnant. Perhaps there's some truth in this – but just to tell an anxious woman that 'all' she has to do is to relax and stop worrying is a very superficial way of helping her with her anxieties.

In recent years, though, partly because of the publicity accorded to the test tube babies research and because of the existence of organisations set up by childless people, the plight of those wanting to, but apparently unable to, conceive has become more apparent, and fertility clinics are more accessible.

STARTING INVESTIGATIONS

If you believe that the time has come when investigations should be undertaken, your GP should refer you to a gynaecologist or to a special subfertility clinic. It's a good idea, though, before you see your own doctor about this, to start to collect exact information which will help her or him to decide whether you need specialist help, and will greatly assist the specialist when you eventually get to the clinic.

First of all, you should keep an exact note of the dates of starting your periods, and how long they last. This will enable you to judge whether they are regular. Then you can keep a temperature chart – most chemists sell these. They also stock 'fertility thermometers' which can be used in conjunction with the chart. The instructions with the chart tell you what to do – you take your vaginal temperature. You'll find that your temperature varies very slightly from day to day, but there should be a clear rise of about 0.4°C just after ovulation. This might be expected around the middle of a regular cycle. Your GP may also agree to arrange for a sperm count to be done on a sample of your partner's semen.

The single woman without a regular partner or the woman hoping to become pregnant by AID may well meet difficulties and opposition from her own GP. If you are in this position you should contact the Women's Reproductive Rights Information Centre, or the British Pregnancy Advisory Service, for advice.

In the UK there is, unfortunately, often a long waiting list for investigation into subfertility, but the above steps might eventually save a little time once you have your appointment. But don't expect quick results, in any case. Because some of the tests have to be done at different times in the menstrual cycle, the investigations can take several months to complete.

The first steps that are usually taken involve a check on whether or not you are ovulating. If you aren't, you may be prescribed drugs which will stimulate the ovaries to produce eggs. At the same time your partner's sperm count will be done. Next you may be asked to have a post-coital test: at the time when you are expected to ovulate you have sexual intercourse shortly before attending the clinic, and a sample of mucus is taken and examined to assess the number and quality of the sperm to be found around the neck of the uterus. Should the sperm be found to be inactive (despite the earlier sperm count having been shown to be normal) it may be suspected that there is something in the mucus that inhibits the activity of the sperm. This can be treated by artificial insemination when the sperm is inserted directly into the uterus. On the other hand, it could be that you were not, in fact, ovulating at the expected time, and a further test may be indicated.

A final test is done by laparoscopy, when the fallopian tubes and other pelvic organs are examined under anaesthetic. A tube through which the organs can be examined is placed through a small puncture in the abdomen. By passing a dye through the tubes any blockage can be seen. If there are adhesions or some other damage to the tubes it is possible that they can be cleared by surgery.

If this and other measures prove unsuccessful, a tiny minority of women may be offered *in vitro* fertilisation. It has to be emphasised that this technique is not only very difficult to get on the NHS or very expensive if done in a private clinic, but that it is really still not fully developed and the failure rate is still high.

WHY ALL THE TESTS?

From the above it can be seen that there are many possible causes of infertility – and indeed some of them are not yet fully understood. Before accepting the need for IVF (*in vitro* fertilisation), it may help to consider what might have been a factor in your particular case. 'Why me?' is a common reaction to any severe health problem. Although in this instance there may be some factor that is beyond your control, or some damage that was done to you or your partner in the past, it's sometimes helpful to know that even at this stage there could be something that might result in the longed-for pregnancy.

It's generally believed that the recent increase in infertility or subfertility may be due to a combination of causes – the tendency to defer pregnancy to an age where fertility is lessened; the possible effects of contraceptive methods used in the past; and the increase of pelvic inflammatory conditions which has arisen in the last decade or so. These factors are examined on page 138.

Some research results published recently even

suggest that smoking might seriously impair a woman's fertility. In the tests, 135 smokers were compared with 543 non-smokers. The study found that smokers had only 67 per cent as much chance of conceiving each cycle as did non-smokers. Moreover, fertility within the group of smokers was related to the number of cigarettes smoked each day. Those who smoked more than twenty a day were just over half as fertile as the non-smokers. Women who smoked fewer than twenty a day were 75 per cent as fertile as non-smokers. The researchers believe that women wishing to become pregnant should be encouraged to give up smoking, as well as those who are already pregnant whose habit could harm their babies.

Clear causes of infertility, however, are:

- Defective sperm – 30 per cent of all cases.
- Failure to ovulate (caused by breakdown of hormonal mechanisms in the pituitary gland) – 30 per cent of all cases.
- Tubal blockage, caused by past infection having damaged the lining of the fallopian tubes – again, 30 per cent of all cases.
- The remaining 10 per cent of infertility cases include sufferers from endometriosis (when the lining of the uterus grows outside it and causes scarring; undeveloped uterus because of hormone deficiencies; 'hostile' mucus in the cervix; and the minority for whom no clear cause can be found.

Any treatment offered after completion of the tests is aimed at correcting treatable deficiencies – it is when treatment fails, but fertilisation is still considered possible, that *in vitro* techniques might be an option.

SHOULD WE REJECT TECHNOLOGY?

Resistance to IVF and other techniques has come from many sides. *In vitro* fertilisation is condemned by some religious groups and by others who believe that such 'unnatural' practices may lead to unacceptable forms of genetic engineering, or that the inevitable destruction of some of the fertilised ova is tantamount to murder. There are feminists, too, who see these developments as yet another example of male technology controlling the lives of women. This case was put very strongly at a conference organised by the Women's Reproductive Rights Campaign in 1986. A statement issued by a group of radical feminists reads in part:

Reproductive technology as it stands now is male controlled. It involves the medical invasion into and experimentation on women without accountability to women. It also involves experimentation on embryos for the development of genetic engineering. The focus in research into genetic engineering is on the elimination of "defects". . . . This can translate into sex, race and class (etc) selective breeding. . . . Reproductive technology has been justified and promoted by the media and medical profession as an issue of helping infertile women and especially of creating new choice for women. To talk about choice without reference to power (control) is at best politically naive. We do not believe that reproductive technologies create real choice (or real control) for women.
All reproductive technologies are by and large too expensive to create real choices for women of all races and all classes. . . .
The way reproductive technology is now put forward reinforces the idea that women without children are incomplete. And in general it is preferred for, if not limited to, white middle class women in "stable" heterosexual relationships.

The statement then goes on to call for more research into the causes of infertility, and its prevention, and for better health care for all women.

On the other hand there are, of course, many women who have made use of technology, or would do so if they had the opportunity, to bring about the birth of a much-wanted baby not possible through 'natural' means. Among these are single women who do not wish to have sexual intercourse with a man and prefer to conceive with sperm from a known or unknown donor. Such women believe that if technology can bring benefits it should be made use of.

Freda McInnis also spoke at the WRRC conference, and she took a very different line. She is a black woman of working class origin. She has had great difficulty in conceiving, because an infection with no symptoms, which must have occurred in her early twenties, seemed to have caused infertility.

'In my early years I was just like many other women in the desire to have children "one day",' said Freda.

'I come from a large family and I desired three or four children. So I was truly mortified when I suspected that something so fundamental could be wrong with me. This was something too horrific and painful to contemplate. Like an ostrich I decided to put off seeing the doctor until I reached thirty – that was the oldest age I could think of. . . .

'Then one day the miracle happened. I was on cloud 109. . . . So I doubt if any of you can understand the disappointment of not only losing the baby but losing the tube; it was an ectopic pregnancy. . . .'

Freda had a bad experience in the hospital – insensitive and demeaning treatment from the doctors. Her longing for a baby increased as one by one her friends announced their pregnancies. Now, as she says:

'I survive by fixating on achieving pregnancy by the test tube method – *my only hope* (official). . . . What is an adequate substitute for motherhood? I refuse to buy a dog or cat. I would go through fire for a baby. . . . Quite simply I and the thousands like me are demanding the right to choose, to choose anything – AID, IVF, surrogacy, any amount of pain – if at the end of it all there is the hope of a pregnancy.'

Since making this powerful plea for a woman's right to choose pregnancy, regardless of the means, Freda has been accepted for the *in vitro* fertilisation programme at an NHS hospital.

'I've been told there's only a one in five chance that it will be successful, but of course I'll take it. I have to wait quite some time before starting with the tests, but at least I feel tremendously relieved that I'm able to take this positive step. I realise I'm lucky – so many women are faced with the choice of private treatment, which they can't possibly afford, or accepting that they'll never have a child. I don't think anyone who hasn't experienced this overwhelming desire to have a baby has any idea what it's like. Women in my position simply can't wait for some future time when research has shown up the causes of infertility and ways of restoring fertility to those who want it.'[*]

An Asian woman now attending a fertility clinic wonders whether there's an element of racism in the attitude of some of the people who oppose reproductive technology:

'I think we may be seen as grabbing the help that is available. This is simply because as a group we tend to ask for help rather younger than some women. It's very important to many Asian women to have babies – if they've been married for several years and they haven't got pregnant they want to know why and to do something about it. We tend not to leave this until we're perhaps over thirty, as English women seem to do.'

She adds bitterly, 'Perhaps at the back of some minds is the feeling that we produce too many children anyway.'

In considering embarking on any treatment for low fertility, it's important to realise that many of the

---

[*] Freda became pregnant as a result of the IVF procedure she underwent late in 1986.

procedures are unpleasant, physically and emotionally, and, most important of all, that the current success rate is very low.

Some women try homoeopathy, acupuncture, naturopathy and other 'alternative' treatments. These may be costly, but in some cases have been known to 'work'. Alternative practitioners look at the 'whole person' to find out what is out of balance and why.

WHAT ABOUT AIDS?

If it is your partner who is infertile, you may think of AID. Since the full-scale and often misleading scare about the AIDS virus has gained so much publicity, women who are considering artificial insemination have been worried about the possible consequences to themselves and their babies of using sperm from a donor. One source of donor sperm has, of course, been gay men. Reports from Australia stated that four women there had come into contact with AIDS when using donor insemination. The donor was gay – a fact that fuelled anti-gay propaganda – but it is known that AIDS is not confined to homosexuals.

It appears that these women had all used the same donor in 1982 – before Australia closed its sperm banks (in 1984). None of the women became pregnant by this donor, and he remains healthy. Three of the women developed AIDS antibodies and the fourth has developed some symptoms of AIDS. All these women were married, with children, and the rest of their families have no signs of AIDS.

This story and the scares surrounding it have obviously concerned many women. It's important to know something about AIDS so that the possible risks can be assessed. It's now accepted that the HIV virus is the 'cause' of AIDS and it is transmitted by direct blood to blood contact; intimate sexual contact; from mother to baby (whether before or after birth is not known). But – and this is what may concern potential recipients of donor sperm – antibodies and the virus have been found in semen. This may be in the sperm or seminal fluid (which, it is not yet known).

At the time of writing the HIV (formerly called HTLV III) test was the main test used – this should show up the presence or otherwise of AIDS antibodies. A positive result means that the virus has been present in the body at some time, but it does not mean that the man actually has AIDS or that he can infect others. Most people found to have AIDS antibodies in their blood stay well, but many will still be carrying the AIDS virus and will probably be infectious to others if they donate blood, organs and semen. Although the test is regarded as reasonably reliable, the Terrence Higgins Trust (the charity that helps AIDS sufferers) has stated that there have been cases of the virus being grown from blood that was antibody negative – up to about 5 per cent of those in whom the virus *is* present have given an antibody negative test result.

The reliability of the test is at least in part influenced by the conditions in which it is done. Anyone having the test done privately must be sure that this is done in a reputable clinic. Since the end of 1985 this should be easier, as facilities at Sexually Transmitted Diseases or Special Clinics have greatly increased. Anyone believing that the AIDS virus or antibodies might be present can go direct to a clinic or ask a GP to arrange for the test.

Although about 75 per cent of gay men with positive test results remain healthy – at least in the short term – about 10 per cent appear to develop AIDS within the following two years, and another 15 per cent develop minor AIDS-related illnesses. Some researchers believe that eventually a majority will develop AIDS. As research advances and more information is available it isn't possible to rule out the likelihood of a cure within a few years. But meanwhile the Terrence Higgins Trust advises men in high-risk groups not to donate sperm – that is, gay or bisexual men, haemophiliacs and men (gay or heterosexual) who have had sexual contact with people in some parts of Africa ('sub-Saharan connections'). The trust's helpline will give more information to telephone callers.

Anyone considering AID from an unknown donor should obviously ensure that the source is, as far as possible, completely reliable. The British Pregnancy Advisory Service has over a hundred donors on its list and all have been screened with the HIV test and the tests for hepatitis B – BPAS believes that these two tests combined give an accurate assessment of whether the donor has, or could develop, AIDS. Most of the donors are heterosexual, young and healthy, and are asked whether they have ever had homosexual contacts. A recent development is the possibility that two screenings will be done, just in case AIDS had been contracted immediately before the test, when it would not show up. By doing the tests twice over, at a three month interval, any risk should be avoided. In July 1986 the DHSS and Royal College of Obstetricians and Gynaecologists suggested that donors should be tested at three-month intervals.

Anyone doing self-insemination must be equally certain that the man donating the sperm is free from AIDS or AIDS antibodies. He should not come from one of the high-risk groups, but it also has to be borne in mind that AIDS is not confined to gay or bisexual men. Clearly this adds greatly to the difficulties of those considering artificial insemination who don't want to use a clinic, as, ideally, a known donor should be asked to take a test, something that many men will not be willing to do if they don't believe themselves to be at risk.

'Women and AIDS' is a booklet produced by the Terrence Higgins Trust in October 1986 – free from the Trust (see page 180). Please enclose a large stamped addressed envelope.

Pointing out that AIDS is now affecting a growing number of women, the booklet warns not only people in 'high-risk' groups, but those contemplating artificial insemination too to make absolutely sure that a donor has been cleared. If proof that the prospective donor is not affected is not forthcoming, it is suggested that his sperm should not be used. The consequences to a woman and her child if the HIV test has not been done could be extremely serious.

For a full discussion of AIDS as it affects women, read the book by Diane Richardson (see page 176).

SURROGATE MOTHERHOOD

A few women who have arranged for others to carry a baby for them (generally the child of the infertile woman's partner) have received some publicity and in 1986 a television serial examined this problem. Condemned by the Warnock Report, and illegal in the UK if the surrogate is paid, the practice may be more widespread than is generally believed. For obvious reasons, figures aren't available.

A SELF-HELP GROUP

Barbara Jane is a member of a self-help group set up by women with problems of fertility. The group was formed with the help of the Women's Reproductive Rights Information Centre, following a conference at which, says Barbara, at least half the participants had been diagnosed as, or believed themselves to be, infertile.

'We've had women as young as twenty and up to the age of about forty two. Some of these women have always known that they were infertile; others have made the painful discovery as a result of investigations after they'd been trying for months or years to conceive. The group gives emotional support. That's terribly important – so many women don't realise how common the problem is. Sharing it makes it easier. But it's a useful source of advice and information. We can tell other women about hopeful new lines of research that we've heard about, the hospitals and clinics where we've found you get the best help or the greatest understanding.

'We meet regularly in central London, but we also do a lot of communicating by telephone. WRRIC, which is the group's meeting place, is also the organisation that women approach in the first place for advice and help, and they give callers the name and telephone number of a group member. Some women find it easier to talk over the 'phone. It's not only the difficulty of getting to a London meeting – it's actually getting out of the house, seeing streets that seem to be full of mothers and babies, passing Mothercare shops. Unless you've experienced it, you can't know how agonising all this can be.

'Every one of us has suffered from insensitivity and unfeeling remarks from other people. Some even congratulate us for not being burdened with children, or assume that we're childless from choice. Parents who want to be grandparents can put enormous pressure on their daughters or sons. Some just won't accept that their children are infertile – they see it as a reflection on *them*, I suppose. Many women who are or have been in the group have had trouble with their marriage or relationships. Many have broken up. A man who wants children and isn't infertile himself eventually leaves his partner for another woman who can produce his child. I remember one very young member of our group saying "Just wait until he realises that I'm never going to have a baby" – she knew that it was simply a matter of time before he left her!'

Barbara Jane says that she tries never to give direct advice to women in the group or who contact her by 'phone. But she does pass on her firm belief – quoted on page 12 – that anyone who's quite sure she wants children shouldn't wait, whatever the apparent obstacles in terms of money, jobs and housing. She also tells how she has personally overcome the anxiety and guilt feelings induced by people who try to 'console' her by saying that she was probably never 'meant' to be a mother.

'It's so easy to cut yourself off from babies and children because it is so painful to see friends' babies when you can't have one yourself. But I think you must overcome this; if you don't, you'll begin to lose confidence in your ability to relate to children and even begin to agree with the idea that you'd be no good as a mother. If I join a group at a party, for instance, where there's a baby, I may feel at first that I just can't bear it. But I march right up and talk to the mother and the baby and cuddle the baby if I can.'

Barbara is firm in her belief that women should stand no nonsense from GPs and consultants. Don't let them fob you off, she says. The time to ask for investigation and help is *when you're worried*, not after some arbitrary period of unsuccessful 'trying'.

Obviously no one is going to rush off for medical help just a month or two after ceasing to use contraception. But someone who has always had irregular periods, has had pelvic infections in the past, or who has some other reason to think that fertility may be a problem, is probably wise to seek help sooner rather than later, and should make sure that she gets it.

The women who meet regularly in the infertility group are never more than about six in number. The good news is that as a result of the help and information they've got from the group, a few do become pregnant and cease to attend for that reason. Others leave because after exploring every possible avenue they eventually come to terms with the fact that they *are* infertile. Then they feel that the group can give them no more, and that it's time to move on and build their lives in a positive way, without children. Others again have found their group so supportive, and believe that they themselves can continue to be of support to new members, so they stay within the group. Passing on their experience, not only of the clinics and medical help that's available, but of the heartbreak of broken relationships and the feelings of personal failure that they're beginning to overcome, can be immensely valuable to other women who are going through the same traumas.

Freda and Barbara clearly feel that for them there's no question of rejecting 'male-dominated' reproductive technology. They'll try every means available. Perhaps the answer lies in women insisting that *they* must make the decisions, that *they* must participate in any procedures used, in an informed manner. There are organisations and self-help groups that can enable women to claim their reproductive rights, and the WRRIC, the blanket organisation listed on page 179, can assist with leaflets and information on this and a number of other issues affecting women.

However, as we've seen, there are many couples who practise full sexual intercourse and still fail to conceive a wanted baby. Procedures for helping these people are described above, but why are some women and men infertile? In the case of women, irregular ovulation, or sometimes no ovulation at all, is to blame. Perhaps ovulation has never been fully established, and this has been masked because the woman has been on the Pill since her teens. Certainly it can take a few months after coming off the Pill to re-establish ovulation, but, if the woman did ovulate regularly before going on to the Pill, she will do so again. If she has never ovulated, this, rather than the Pill, is the problem.

Then, as we've seen, damage or blockage to the fallopian tubes is another very common reason for failure to conceive, and this can be caused by an infection such as chlamydia which may never have shown itself in any other way. Endometriosis is another condition that could affect the tubes. Cervical infections and mucus which act against the sperm are other possibilities.

It's obviously important that a woman showing signs of infection of any of the pelvic organs should get treatment, as should her partner. Irritation, pain, heavy or unusual discharge are symptoms that should be investigated.

Male infertility can also be caused by genital infections which may permanently obstruct the sperm ducts, or by damage to the penis, testicles or vas deferens. Sperm production could be affected by certain diseases – the best known being mumps which affects the sperm of a minority of adolescent boys or men. Impotence, for whatever reason, is obviously a cause of failure of the partner to conceive.

MISCARRIAGE AND STILLBIRTH

There are some women who have no difficulty in becoming pregnant, but fail to carry the baby to full term. Until recently it has always been assumed that the reason for miscarriage was that it was 'nature's way' of rejecting a damaged foetus. This may well be the reason why some women miscarry, and it seems to be confirmed by the fact that very many of them go on to produce normal, healthy babies born at the 'right' time. But there must be other explanations for those women who miscarry repeatedly. In some cases a so-called 'incompetent cervix' is to blame, and this can be dealt with by the insertion of a stitch under general anaesthetic, which keeps the cervix closed until it is removed when the birth is due.

Recently another reason for repeated miscarriage has been discovered. It has been found that some women's immune systems reject the 'foreign body' – the foetus – just as if it were a form of infection or an implanted alien organ. The cure for this condition is an injection of cells from the partner before the pregnancy is started. The woman is thus immunised against the 'invader' and the pregnancy goes ahead normally. So far only a small number of women have been able to take advantage of this technique, developed in St Mary's Hospital in London, but it is such a comparatively simple one that we might hope that its availability could be extended.

There are many reasons for stillbirth, and this and neo-natal death are becoming rarer as women take greater care of their health in pregnancy and modern technology helps in the management of difficult births. Many women feel, quite understandably, that they don't want to be wired up to machines, forced to have their babies in over-mechanised conditions and with little or no say in what is happening to them. When everything is going normally, it can seem absurd to apply high-tech to an essentially natural process. However, there seems little doubt that many babies' – and mothers' – lives have been saved in the minority of cases when things *do* go wrong. It's for this reason that mothers opposed to too much technology often decide that they will negotiate beforehand just how much – if any – is to be used at the birth if everything is normal, but will arrange to be in a hospital where it is available in an emergency.

Anyone who experiences the loss of a much-wanted baby either in pregnancy or through stillbirth suffers a bereavement, but it's only quite recently that it's been recognised as something as intensely emotionally painful as the loss of an older child. In the past some women who suffered such a loss tried to put it all behind them, blocking off their natural grief. They weren't helped by doctors who 'consoled' them by a breezy 'better luck next time' or relatives who pointed out that they had many more years of childbearing before them. The scars of unexpressed grief can last a lifetime. There are now organisations (see page 180) that can help with counselling and support, made up of women who have suffered similar loss. They understand how deep and bitter is the pain in someone who has planned and looked forward to happy parenthood but whose hopes are cruelly thwarted.

CAN YOU ADJUST?

As we've seen, there are many reasons why you could fail to produce the child you've decided you want. If you're determined about it, you may have gone through all sorts of time consuming, worrying and even painful procedures – to no avail.

But the time may come when you have to decide that enough is enough. You've made all possible enquiries and you've been to all the experts and the reluctant conclusion has to be that the situation is irremediable and you won't be able to have that baby. This is a very hard thing to accept, and coming to terms with this loss is something that's going to take time. If you haven't done so before, you may now decide to seek the help of an organisation for childless people (see page 180). Local groups of people in the same position as yourself may provide you with the support you need, the reassurance that it is possible to build your lives on different foundations from the ones you expected, and to aim your energies in another direction.

WHAT ABOUT ADOPTION?

It's taken a long time for the current facts about adoption to sink into the public consciousness. Twenty or more years ago a couple wanting children but unable to produce them themselves were advised to adopt a baby. And although there were often problems along the way, in many cases this turned out to be a solution to the disappointment of childlessness, as well as providing a better future for an orphaned or disadvantaged child. Today the whole situation has changed.

For many reasons there are fewer babies needing adoptive parents – single parenthood is much more readily accepted by society, and abortion in certain cases is legal, so that fewer unwanted babies are born, for instance. The greatest change has been a shift on the part of the social work agencies from a position where adoption was seen as primarily something that conveniently met the needs of childless couples, to the present outlook – that the needs of the child must come first. Consequently, not only is there a great drop in the number of babies available for adoption, but many couples who would previously have had no difficulty in getting through the 'vetting' procedure are now rejected as potential parents.

This can cause great bitterness. As many couples who have been turned down will say, social workers don't come along and investigate the suitability to become parents of those who are able to produce their own children. The consequence, they point out, is that a baby can be born to a rejecting mother or a battering father, and no one asks any questions until the child's trouble becomes a matter of concern to family, neighbours and social workers. All this when some apparently blameless, caring people aren't accepted for the would-be adopters lists, without being told just why. And, although adoption agencies now do accept – sometimes – single people as potential adopters, in many cases this does not include lesbian couples or gay men.

So, since the early 1970s, it's been very hard to find a *baby* for adoption. At first, though, it seemed that there were plenty of older children of 'mixed race' available – children who had been languishing in children's homes for several years and desperately needed new parents. Many were successfully placed with white families; but as they grew up problems of identity arose and it gradually became clear that in general, success with such children was much more likely if they were adopted by black parents. Pressure from the black community and from the increasing numbers of black social workers meant that many more black parents came forward anxious to adopt. Adoption of black children by white parents became rarer – adoption of whites by blacks, of course, was never a 'problem', because it just didn't happen.

There are, however, other older children who await adoption – those who are handicapped mentally or physically or who are regarded as disturbed and difficult to handle in an ordinary family setting. Although those working with these children agree that ideally they need to be living out of the institutions now holding them, it's felt that they present too much of a challenge to be adopted by someone who doesn't regard caring for them as a full-time job. Consequently some of these children and adolescents are placed for adoption in homes where the chief carer (normally the woman) is paid for her work in looking after them, and who regards this job as a full-time salaried one, comparable to any other kind of social work. Professional social workers offer continued support in such cases, and in some areas adoptive parents have formed groups to air their problems and discuss solutions with people experiencing similar difficulties.

The BAAF booklet listed on page 176 gives all the necessary preliminary information for anyone considering adopting a child in the 1980s.

Fostering is another option for someone who feels she has something to offer a child in need – long- and short-term foster parents are needed. The local social services department is probably only too anxious to contact people willing to offer this service to children in its care.

SOMEONE ELSE'S CHILD?

It may be that you are unable to have a child of your own, but that your partner already has a child or children from a previous relationship. Wicked stepmothers are so much part of folklore that anyone undertaking to be a mother to her partner's daughter or son tends to question her ability to fill the role without trouble. It certainly can be a difficult and demanding one, and if, at the same time, she finds that she is unable to bear a child herself the situation may be even harder to handle. Once more, though, a self-help group may come to the rescue – the one listed on page 180 was formed a few years ago – and its members can offer help, advice, and the chance to let off steam, because they, too, have been going through the same sort of experiences. The books listed on page 177 also draw largely on personal experience to offer help and comfort to anyone going through a difficult patch with stepchildren.

A CHILD'S DEATH

If infertility is a major worry in the mind of someone who hasn't yet become pregnant, and wonders whether she will be able to conceive, the possibility, however faint, that her child might die in infancy or later is a natural concern. Both situations involve a profound sense of loss, and it is pointless and heartless to balance one against the other.

Most good baby books address these problems, and there are organisations and self-help groups covering stillbirth, neo-natal death and the death of older children (see page 180). Although a woman facing stillbirth or the death of her baby immediately after birth may be tempted to try to suppress the grief and pretend to herself that the experience she has been through was more like an illness or an operation than the birth of her child, the experience of mothers who have suffered such losses does show that acknowledgment of what has happened, seeing the baby and accepting it, has an ultimately healing effect. No one should try to 'encourage' any bereaved mother by telling her that she can easily have another child. The one she has lost is irreplaceable. It follows that it is unlikely to be a good idea to try to become pregnant immediately after the loss; time must be allowed for the grief to be worked through. Still less is it wise to see the later baby as a substitute for the first. She or he is a person in their own right and can't fulfil the needs of the parents by being a 'replacement'.

We'll look now at another decision that faces many parents – should they have a second child?

CHAPTER 10

ANOTHER CHILD?
COULD YOU COPE WITH MORE?

Many women deciding to take the plunge into pregnancy are simultaneously deciding on a future that not only involves one baby, but another one, two or more. The desire for a family rather than just one ('only') child is overriding. Facts, myths and strong feelings intermingle to persuade you that if you're going to have one child, you'd better – or at least might as well – have more.

How do 'only' children feel about their parents' decision to limit the family to just one child? Young children, of course, often yearn for a younger sister or brother and feel cheated when one isn't forthcoming. But this – often a passing phase – doesn't seem to be a good enough reason for parents to oblige: they, after all, will be the ones with a responsibility that could re-shape their own lives. Once again, grandparents and friends may start to pressurise – on the only child's behalf.

'My mother tells me I'm being selfish not to give my daughter a playmate,' says a thirty year-old:

'She says I had no right to have a first child without planning for a second – I'm depriving Julie of something very valuable. If she doesn't learn to share and take turns in the family, she'll grow up self-centred and unconcerned about the needs of other people. I do worry about that.'

Adults who have been only children vary in their

perceptions of the disadvantages and advantages of being a singleton. Someone living in an isolated hamlet, far from cousins and at too great a distance from her school to make out-of-school contacts easily will suffer much more from loneliness than a child with a strong neighbourhood play-life and a home where visiting relatives are part of the scenery. The first may say, when she's an adult, that she did have a hard time adjusting when she first left home for work or further education. The second will say that she never missed companionship, and the privileges she got as an only child far outweighed any possible disadvantage.

Some adult singletons add that they did feel pressurised as children by parents who had put all their eggs into one basket.

'The relationship was too intense. I felt watched all the time, never able to do anything without checking with my mother. If she'd had more children she couldn't have concentrated so fiercely on me. It's taken me a long time to break the dependence I've always felt on her approval or disapproval of myself and any action I was taking.'

That's the reaction of someone who has made a firm decision to have at least two children herself, lest the pattern reasserts itself in her own family.

A middle-aged man who was an only child points to another disadvantage he feels he's suffering:

'My parents are getting old and they have a number of health problems. They're totally dependent on me and my wife for day-to-day check-ups on how they are. I was offered a good job some hundreds of miles away. I felt I couldn't take it in the circumstances. If there'd been brothers or sisters we could have shared the responsibility.'

But another feels that as a child he gained very much from being the only child in the family. His parents were able to devote their limited resources to him, giving him opportunities of foreign travel, music lessons, providing him with books and educational experiences they could never have offered if they'd had other children. 'And they had more time for me,' he says. 'I think that's even more important.'

Taking all the factors into account, there's no way of deciding that the one-, two- or three-child family is best. For every singleton who would love to have a sister or brother, there's probably another child who quarrels incessantly with her sibs and will admit to hating the sight of them; in some cases dislike persists into adulthood, though it's perhaps more common for reconciliation to take place once the family has grown up.

So we're back where we started. The decision to have another child has to be made on the basis of the parents' needs and attitudes and personal goals – just as the decision to have the first baby was.

Probably the deciding factor will be the way the parents feel about their existing situation. A single parent will weigh up the difficulties she's already facing in trying to bring up a child without much back-up and may realise that she'd find it even more difficult to cope with two. Someone whose partner has taken an adequate share in the upbringing of one child could expect him or her to do so with more. An extended family living nearby or a network of friends should be able to provide further reciprocated help.

Someone who has good child-minding arrangements to enable her to go to work will probably find that two children can be as easily cared for as one. On the other hand, if she's had to give up work because child-minding has proved unsatisfactory, she may not be eager to prolong her period of 'unemployment' by having another child. If managing alone has been stressful, for whatever reason, and there's no likelihood of change, it would seem sensible to consider whether further responsibility might not turn out to be just too much. If it's right to resist outside pressure when it's a question of having *one* baby, it's certainly even more reasonable to refuse to be pressurised when experience tells you that another would be in no one's interest.

Just as some women are motivated to have a child because something is going wrong in their lives – unhappiness at work, unsatisfactory relationships or some other cause for discontent – so is a woman who has opted to make her child her main interest in life. She may worry that with her or his growing independence she'll be left without a focus. Admits one mother:

'Ideally I'd have a never-ending succession of babies. I sometimes dream of having such a large family that by the time my youngest started school my eldest would be making me a grandmother! I'm afraid it isn't so much that I love children – though I do love my own – but that I never really found myself in any other role. I've been at home so long that the thought of re-training and going into the world of work just daunts me too much. Of course my dream isn't realistic, and I'll have to face up to the fact that I can't hide my fears of facing the outside world forever behind the excuse that I'm needed at home.'

But you may decide on much more rational grounds that you want a second child. Now arises yet another dilemma! When?

TIMING IT RIGHT

There are those who believe that the closer the children in a family are in age, the happier they'll be, and that the parents too, will get all the 'difficult bits' over all at once. Giving up work for five or seven years may be a lot easier than doing so twice over in the same space of time, and then for a longer period. On the other hand, there's a lot to be said for having an older child settled in nursery or primary school before having another baby. Perhaps the decision to have two close together is forced upon you because if you waited too long for your second child, you might be rather old for a safe and healthy pregnancy. But although in many ways it's rather convenient to have a baby and a toddler to care for at the same time, the job can be very demanding. At eighteen months or twenty months old the elder child may not take too kindly to the presence of the new baby who takes up so much of her mother's time and attention, and full responsibility for two demanding, exhausting little creatures can prove too much – you really do need to share the load. Once the children are older, though, there's a strong possibility that despite the odd rows and jealousies, they will enjoy each other's company most of the time, and thus take some of the stress off the parents.

At three, four or five the older child's horizons have already expanded and she's not so dependent on your undivided attention. She may even get a lot of pleasure out of helping with a baby, and she'll probably be spending part of her day at a playgroup or nursery class, giving you more time to talk to her and play with her when you're both free. And because your body will have had more time to recover after childbirth and breast-feeding, you have more energy to spread between work and family.

No one can decide these pros and cons for you – but if you and your partner can come to an agreement bearing in mind all the factors that might apply in your particular case, there's a greater chance that your decision will turn out to have been the right one – for you.

THE TWO-FAMILY FAMILY

In the last chapter we touched briefly on the question of step-parenting. Being a stepchild is now so common that it's almost approaching the norm for a child to find her or himself suddenly presented with a ready-made family of brothers and sisters – perhaps as unlike themselves as it's possible to be, and certainly with a different background and life-experience. Books on the problems of step-parents have been written (see page 177) and these include accounts of the difficulties such children may face – told in their own words.

There must be very few families in which jealousies between sisters and brothers don't arise. Most parents have experienced complaints from each of their children that it's the sister or brother who is preferred to themselves – 'it's not fair' being a universal complaint. So it's hardly surprising that a child asked to accept a new brother or sister into her family, possibly very near her own age, is going to look out for the real or imaginary preferences on the part of the 'incoming' parent. Agencies arranging adoptions are careful to avoid placing a child in a family where there's a child of similar age, and for good reason. Children are much readier to accept a new baby than someone who is seen as a rival. One adult remembers:

'My sister was always the baby of the family and I didn't see her as nearly so much of a threat as my stepsister when she arrived when we were both about eight. She was prettier and cleverer than I was and my father seemed to prefer her to me. Looking back I realise he was probably bending over backwards to make sure that she felt as welcomed and loved as his other two girls. But at the time it seemed to me that I got blamed for anything that went wrong and that I was expected – unreasonably I felt – to be accepting and understanding beyond my years. We were grown up with children of our own before we really became good friends – there was so much resentment on my part and so much defensiveness on hers.'

In other families it takes the birth of a baby to the new partnership to unite stepsisters and brothers. 'When my baby brother was born I began to feel that we were a real family despite our different origins,' is how another woman sums up her childhood experience.

A childless woman accepting her partner's ready-made family doesn't have these particular problems to contend with, but she does have the wicked stepmother image to combat, and however well intentioned she is she may suffer at the children's hands from comparisons with their 'real' mother, to whom death or distance may have lent enchantment. Particularly if she's keen to have a baby, she may be unwilling to wait while she builds, patiently and lovingly, a good relationship with her stepchildren. It may be that in her case, too, having a baby will unite the family, but this is something that needs careful consideration by both partners, who have not only the usual considerations of timing, availability of support and other factors this book has examined. It could be that a decision to wait until the older children are maturer and more understanding of their parents' needs would pay off. If those children have been through a difficult time when their mother died or their parents split up, they may need time to rebuild their confidence in the new partnership and themselves.

Grandparents in these situations can play an important part. Obviously it may be difficult for paternal grandparents to accept that their former daughter-in-law has not only rejected their son, but foisted a new father on the children. It can be asking a lot of them to expect them to maintain the same sort of relationship as they've always had with the grandchildren and those children's mother. Some, accepting that the children's well-being is more important than any reservations they may have about the new relationship, continue to involve themselves as fully as circumstances allow. And it would be wise, for the children's sake, to encourage contact. 'I've got lots of grandparents,' one little girl explains:

'I suppose I like the old ones best, and I go and stay with the ones at the seaside as well as the ones in London. But I see my new grandma when she comes to visit all of us, and she takes us out to interesting places. I like that. We don't see much of the grandparents who're abroad, but they do send us lovely letters, and birthday presents for me as well as the others.'

This child sees an extra set of grandparents as a bonus rather than a cause of conflict.

Active and accessible grandparents can provide not only the traditional grandparenting back-up to the family, but an emotional support to children who may be troubled by the new situation into which their parents' needs have thrown them. Unless they're openly hostile and likely to exacerbate family problems, continuing contacts must be good.

TIMES ARE CHANGING

Variations and permutations of traditional and new forms of parenthood will develop as the twentieth century comes towards its end. There's every indication that increased independence and assertion of their rights will enable women to make decisions about the way they and their children live, and that this will involve patterns of continuing change. We're not quite as far from the old two-parent, two-children family and its inheritance of Victorian values as we may like to think. As long as power is vested in male institutions, women who want to be free to choose are going to have a difficult time. The odds are against them. But not impossibly so. The solution to the problems of being a mother, both in the short and the long-term, lies in the support and inspiration of other women. Countless numbers are finding that the loneliness and isolation that has been a feature of motherhood for the last hundred years is giving way to a new kind of life in which children will cease to be a burden as well as a joy. Sharing and caring with other women – whatever the obstacles – will provide the key.

If you're absolutely sure that you want to have a baby – or more than one – you can skip the next chapter. But what about those who are unsure, or who've decided never to be mothers? Reading on might help.

CHAPTER 11

CHILDLESS BY CHOICE
CAN YOU BE HAPPY WITHOUT CHILDREN?

An eight year-old explains why she doesn't want to grow up and have children of her own. 'It's all the *arranging*', she says.

The life-style of her family illustrates what she means. It will be familiar to many parents – the 'you pick up Jenny from her music lesson and I'll get the dinner on so that you can get out to your meeting, and would you remember to pay the paper bill and remind me to take Liz's shoes to be mended tomorrow, and do you think we could ask next-door to take in that parcel I'm expecting, and could you be here on Thursday morning because the gas man's coming?' syndrome. Yes, her parents do spend a lot of time *arranging*, because they both go out to work, they're both conscientious about giving their children time and attention, and organising their lives is really almost a full-time job in itself. Added to the stresses they both experience at work they're faced with a timetable that has to be *arranged* from day to day so that there's always someone at home to see the children off to school and be there when they get back. Illness and school holidays can involve further complicated and sometimes expensive *arrangements*.

Do parents like this sometimes wonder whether they did the right thing when they decided to have children? Do they envy their childless friends who have time for jobs, hobbies, further education, political action, exciting holidays, the chance to go to a concert or theatre, spend an evening in the pub or out dancing, and even a weekend away on impulse? If they do, they seldom admit to it. Because within some limitations they are able to share most of the chores and most of the problems. Between them they've got (just about) enough back-up to meet most of the demands upon them. And difficult as life is at times, there are enough rewards to make them glad they did undertake their onerous job. As each year passes the children are able to take greater responsibility for themselves and take a greater share in running the house, they become more independent, more mature in their ideas, more equal and more interesting. And strong family bonds remain.

But what of the single or divorced woman who has no one with whom to share the care of her children? In earlier chapters the prime need for adequate and consistent back-up and sharing emerged. Some of the single women quoted earlier and in Jean Renvoize's *Going Solo* speak eloquently of their difficulties when they struggle on as sole carers. If the presence of children causes considerable stress on a two-parent working family, it's obvious that the difficulties are going to be a lot worse for a woman on her own.

It must have been appreciation of this probability that caused the women in an American group set up to discuss whether or not they should have children to decide that after all, they wouldn't. As reported by Jean Renvoize, 'most of the women attending the Single Mothers by Choice "thinkers" groups decide not to have children after they have been presented with all the facts.'

These are single women, and their decision does conflict with the experience of the many other single women quoted in *Going Solo* who are glad that they did become pregnant. They don't minimise the difficulties, and many of them, of course, were able to arrange help from friends or afford regular paid help with small children. Those who were not so fortunate, as the book points out, were less sure about the rightness of their decision. But they were in a minority.

But what about the woman in a marriage or a stable relationship – with a man or a woman – who still decides that motherhood is not for her? As we've seen, although career interruption, difficulties in fitting in all the things she wants to do with her life and fears about the long-term prospects for the partnership may be factors, there are many women who just don't want children. Full stop. They may like children – as long as they're not theirs. They may even have jobs connected with children. But the idea of producing a child of their own just doesn't appeal.

That's a very personal decision and, of course, one that ideally should be taken with the partner concerned very early on in the relationship. Personal as it is, though, unfortunately carrying out this decision is a very public act. Earlier we saw how some would-be grandparents try to pressurise younger people into producing a family, but the pressure comes from other quarters, too.

'I'm amazed at the way some of our friends start hinting, and finally propagandising us about having a baby. It's as though our decision to be childless was some sort of attack on them. My husband even had crude jokes made about it at work – suggestions that he didn't know how, and offers to come home with him and show him.'

Another woman says she eventually decided to shut people up by telling them there was something wrong with her tubes – only to be showered with suggestions that she should go to a fertility clinic or try for a test tube baby.

The horror that someone should make a conscious decision to remain childless is only exceeded by the outrage felt by the same sort of people when a woman elects to have a baby without a male partner.

If those who are childless because of problems with their fertility feel the need of counselling and support groups, the much-maligned couples who *choose* not to have children are also in need of help. It was to meet this need that some years ago groups of people in this position broke away from the original group of childless people, which had consisted of those who wanted children and had been unable to have them, as well as people who had elected not to become parents. It was obviously an uneasy partnership and relationships within it could become as bitter as the situation in a hospital ward where women who have had stillbirths are placed next to those who have had an abortion. As a result of the breakup of the original organisation, an association of child-*free* as distinct from child*less* people was formed.

Reference was made earlier in this book (see page 18) to this association of people who have decided not to have children. As we saw, much of their published material is concerned with the decision-making stage, but they do also provide support for individuals and couples who have already made up their minds that parenthood is not right for them. The address of BON (British Organisation of Non-Parents) will be found on page 180.

Ideally the decision about having children should have been made early in a couple's relationship. It can happen, however, that one or other partner has a change of mind.

A MAN'S VIEW

'One of the most attractive things about Marie was her love of children,' says Jerry:

'I saw her with my sister's baby and she seemed so totally maternal. We talked about having children of our own, and she seemed to agree that we would – it was just a question of "when". We've been together now for some years, but the decision has kept on being put off. Finally I confronted her with this constant postponement and she admitted that she didn't think now that she could go through with it. She makes all sorts of excuses – she calls them reasons – such as fear of nuclear war, uncertainty about employment, whether she'd be able to cope – that sort of thing. I say that where there's a will there's a way, so I can only assume that the will is lacking. I feel absolutely let down, and it does make me question our whole relationship. We're both very unhappy.'

With other couples this situation is reversed. One question that agony aunts meet over and over again – and it applies to many other aspects of a couple's relationship – is the perennial 'will he change?' 'If we marry . . . if we have a baby . . . if we move . . .': in a whole range of problems women experience in their relationships they want to know whether they can influence their partner to change so that he will agree to comply with *their* needs and wishes. Of course change is possible – we all change as we mature – but it may be asking too much to expect someone who has firmly-entrenched and well-thought-out reasons for doing or not doing something to reverse completely his beliefs and behaviour to comply with a partner's wishes.

'I did hope that when we'd settled down and life was a little easier he'd decide that after all we should have children. But this hasn't happened. He just says that if I want a baby I should go ahead, but that I must not expect him to welcome my decision – or the baby. It really puts a pistol at my head. I want to stay with him, but if I do, it means I won't have children, because I can't see that it would be fair to a child to have an uninterested father. I know now that it's no use hoping that once we had a child he'd change his mind. He isn't that sort of person. I really can't blame him – it was my fault that I expected him to change to my way of thinking; he'd made his attitude perfectly clear right from the beginning. I think our marriage is strong enough to weather this, though. Other couples are childless and seem quite happy, and I think we can be, once I accept that we'll never have a baby.'

This woman is now looking for a way to change her job so that she works with young children; and she says that she does get a lot of pleasure out of her contact with nephews and nieces.

Anyone who has made the decision that she will never want children, but who does have, and wants to continue with, heterosexual relationships is most likely to think about sterilisation as an option. 'If you're really quite sure that you don't want a baby, it seems futile to continue with contraception,' says a thirty year-old social worker:

'Despite my doctor's assurances, I'm not too happy with the possible long-term effects of the Pill. As I'm a smoker – I've failed over and over again to give it up – I'd have to change the method soon, anyway, and there are disadvantages, I think, about the other contraceptive methods. I'm seriously considering getting sterilised.'

At the end of this chapter there is a discussion on sterilisation, but, since you must assume that sterilisation can't be reversed, you may feel, like another woman in her early thirties who has been thinking about it, that you'd need to be extremely sure about yourself and your relationships before taking such a serious step:

'I love the man I'm with, but we do have our ups and downs, and I see so many of our friends and colleagues breaking up that even though I don't *think* it will happen to us, I suppose it might. I don't *think* I'd get involved in the same way with someone else – but there again, I might. And I might then be surer about committing myself to having a child. I want to keep the option open, however unlikely it seems at the moment.'

Although she knows that there's little evidence that female or male sexuality can be adversely affected, she wonders about the emotional impact if either of them were sterilised. 'I can't help feeling that I'd experience the loss of that option as something hard to take.' She's also concerned that some (as yet inconclusive) evidence has been published that shows that women who have been sterilised may have heavier and more frequent periods. Her partner firmly refuses to consider a vasectomy because there have been reports that vasectomised monkeys have an increased risk of heart disease!

As we shall see, if either you or your partner have been sterilised, it's very likely that you won't be able to change your minds later. If you haven't taken that step, it's always possible that circumstances may change in such a way that having a baby is not only a possibility, but something you now really want. Earlier in this book we looked back at the pros and cons of having a baby when you're 'elderly', and it's worth repeating the points made there. Briefly, there's little doubt that with increasing age it becomes rather more difficult to conceive, though a healthy couple should be successful sooner or later; there is increased risk of foetal abnormality, again increasing slightly with each year of maternal age; and a woman in her late thirties or early forties may find the whole business of pregnancy and motherhood more of a strain than someone in her twenties would.

Most women who consider sterilisation do so after years on the Pill or with the coil, or having used barrier methods. Conscientiously and correctly used, these methods are very effective, but they have their disadvantages. They are, however, reversible, and anyone thinking she *might* want to have a baby should continue to use the best method for *her*.

This book is not about contraception. For a full discussion of all types of contraception, with a critical look at the disadvantages as well as the advantages, see *Contraception: a Practical and Political Guide* by Rose Shapiro (1987).

**A FIRM
DECISION**

We've seen the difficulties faced by many women and men when making a final decision not to have children. Others who have decided to remain childless, and have carried out their decision, are worth listening to.

Janet decided, after a series of unsatisfactory relationships, that she would concentrate on her career, which she knew would continue to give her satisfaction. Now forty, she thinks she made the right decision:

'Life's never perfect. If I had found the right partner I probably would have had children. But I just don't know whether I'd have been happier as a mother than as a professional person. I doubt whether I could have done both jobs really well. Who can possibly say what would have happened? I enjoy my job, I can plan my life as I want to, there's no one to tie me down. When I think of the lives that some of my friends are leading – sticking to an unsatisfactory marriage "for the sake of the children" or just as bad, struggling through separation and divorce and then having to cope with all sorts of problems, with no proper job and hardly any money, I'm really thankful that I didn't run the risk. Some of these friends tell me how much they envy me, how sensible they think I was. Yes, I'm lonely at times and yes, I do sometimes get involved with an "unsuitable" man and that can be painful. But I do recover, and there are only two people affected, not three, and one of them a defenceless child. "If in doubt, don't" is a sensible motto, I think.'

Another woman, also in her forties but married, isn't so sure that she made the right choice. When she decided not to have a baby she was very happy and successful in her job, in a highly competitive field. She didn't believe it possible to combine this career with motherhood, because she felt that a child is entitled to her mother's time and attention and shouldn't be handed over to other people to bring up.

But now things have gone sour – government cuts have resulted in a shrinkage of personnel and opportunities in the research field where she was such a high-flier.

'I'm completely blocked now. Unless there's a drastic change I'll never be able to do the sort of work I wanted. It's too late to think about having a baby. If I'd known this would happen, I'd have acted differently. We're now beginning to think seriously about adoption. If we were able to adopt I think I'd be willing to give up my job or at any rate work part-time.'

In complete contrast is the attitude of her contemporary, a comprehensive-school teacher. She's glad to have made the decision, early in her relationship with her present husband, that they wouldn't have children.

'Friends pity me, I think. They hint that we'll have a bleak old age, with no close family, no grandchildren, no stake in the future. I can't see that happening. There are so many people and causes we're interested in, things we can expect to absorb us fully well into old age. What guarantee would we have had that our relationship with our children would have been good, that they would live near us and want us to be involved with our grandchildren? After all, we ourselves emigrated here and left our parents behind. We didn't quarrel with them, but we weren't all that close. That can happen in any family, and if it's happened once in ours it could have happened again. I'd rather be dependent on *myself* when I'm old, not a younger generation.'

Sandy Jaffee, an American woman film maker currently directing a film about older, childless women's lives, reports that not one of the women she interviewed for her film and the book she is writing regretted her childless state. Some of these older women were childless by choice, though others had failed to conceive despite their intention to become pregnant. All felt that they had led satisfying lives as non-parents. This observation is borne out by the findings of American researchers Glen and McLanahan in a study of women over fifty. They found no difference in happiness or satisfaction between mothers and childless women, regardless of their income or whether or not they were employed. The authors' conclusion was:

'The best evidence now available indicates that the present young adult should not choose to have children on the basis of expectations that parenthood will lead to psychological rewards in the later stages of life. The prospects for such rewards seem rather dim at best.'

Earlier some of the many reasons for uncertainty about parenthood were examined. One overriding factor is a woman's perception of herself as 'mother-material'. One child-free woman explains:

'Of course my main reason for not wanting children is that I feel I'm simply not cut out for motherhood. I'm impatient; I get bored if I'm not out and about, seeing immediate results for my efforts. I'm not saying that raising a child isn't important – obviously it is. All I do say is that I really wouldn't be a good mother, and I don't see why I should produce a child who might be emotionally deprived, because I couldn't give it the attention and affection that I do believe wanted children get and need. Selfish? That's what some people have told me, but actually I think I'm the opposite, in admitting that I'm not the right person to be a mother, and sticking to this decision.'

WHAT ABOUT STERILISATION? This woman has now been sterilised. 'What's the point of continuing with contraception which may be dangerous or inconvenient or both?' she asks.

'As I'm married and in my early thirties I had a difficult job convincing the gynaecologist that I really did want sterilisation. They don't give you credit for being able to make up your mind, and tell you all sorts of stories about women who were sterilised and then decided they'd made a mistake and came back to have the sterilisation reversed – which is generally impossible. "You may be very sorry you took this step," they tell you. Well, I believe that if I make mistakes in my life, I have to take the consequences. Who hasn't had to live with the results of some past mistake? To my mind it would be a mistake for me to have had a baby and not only I but the *child* would have had to live with that mistake.'

More and more women and men are opting for sterilisation – 22 per cent of people of both sexes of 'reproductive age' in 1984. But although women quite rightly object to the paternalistic approach of some doctors who insist that they don't know their own minds, it *is* necessary to approach the idea with caution, and after consideration of the possible outcomes. Women may find a nurse or health visitor helpful as a counsellor.

It's important to know what the facts really are. It is not true, for instance, that sterilisation is invariably irreversible. But on the other hand, since the success rate in attempts to reverse the results of sterilisation is low, it would be very unwise indeed to assume that if you changed your mind later, everything could be put back together again and you could have a child. It is also wise to take account of the figures that show a failure rate of one in 300 for female sterilisation and one in 1,000 for men. Not high: but maybe the result of failure – pregnancy – in your particular case could be devastating. And your partner who decides to have a vasectomy should bear in mind that he will still be fertile for some weeks after the operation, so contraception must be continued until his semen is found, on a follow-up test, to be clear of sperm.

Neither male or female sterilisation is a particularly

serious operation and in both cases local anaesthetics are the norm. Women now usually have to stay in hospital or clinic only on a day-care basis, while for men it's an even shorter procedure. Some men complain of great soreness for a few days afterwards, but this is seldom bad enough to be incapacitating. Female sterilisation by tubal ligation involves sealing off the fallopian tubes, by cutting, tying with sutures or clips, or by the application of heat (cauterisation). This can usually be done under local anaesthetic: a very small incision in the abdomen enables a surgical tube to be inserted (laparoscopy). Minor discomfort when the anaesthetic wears off can be expected.

Research by obstetrician Wendy Savage underlines the point that it is very undesirable for a woman to have a sterilisation at the same time as she is undergoing an abortion, or childbirth or some other surgical procedure. If it is suggested to you that 'we might as well tidy everything up' at the same time – don't be pressurised. Savage found that if there was an interval of about six or more months between the birth, caesarean section or abortion and the sterilisation, fewer than 1 per cent of women regretted having had the sterilisation. If it was done without interval, between 10 and 25 per cent later said that they regretted it.

It has even happened that sterilisation has been done without the woman's consent ('in her own best interests,' of course) and that the woman hasn't even been told that she was sterilised. So if there's any likelihood of your being in a position where someone might press you to be sterilised while you are in a vulnerable state for some other reason – refuse, saying firmly that you need more time to think.

It's not usual for doctors to consent readily to sterilisation for someone of childbearing age who hasn't already had children, so if you are really determined to have the operation you may have to try several doctors before you get one to agree. In one study of women who had been sterilised, 40 per cent had been refused previously. It is possible to have sterilisation performed privately, but obviously this can be costly, and would probably be considered only by someone who had met with difficulties.

There's one thing that all these women agree about – deciding never to have children, and confirming this decision by being sterilised, is not something that most people can or should contemplate in their early twenties. It would be only if the strong probability that a child would suffer from some serious hereditary disease were to influence the decision, they believe, that a really young woman should consider this step. Contraceptive methods may not be ideal, but they do provide the opportunity for second thoughts.

Just as some women feel that they were wise to postpone having children until they felt they were mature enough to be parents, others are glad that they didn't make an irrevocable decision never to become pregnant too early. At the beginning of this book the point was made that many women who were active in the feminist movement in their early twenties, and felt at that time that children would never be part of their lives, have thought again as they reached the 'crucial age' of thirty plus.

There's no last word. All we can say is that for the majority of women who have made a carefully thought-out decision not to have children it's been the right one. As with any other decision, there may be times when they question it, look for a while at the 'might-have-been' with some regret – and then get on with the lives they have chosen.

CHAPTER 12

BACK TO YOU

Look back to the beginning of this book. It was pointed out right from the start that your decision about having or not having a baby was just about the hardest one you'd ever have to make. And of course if you'd already made your mind up, one way or the other, you wouldn't have bothered to read this book. But you were uncertain, subject to so many conflicting views and advice. On pages 102–8 we tried to sum up your feelings after reading Part One and it's to be hoped that the way you responded to the questions on those pages clarified most of the issues raised earlier, and enabled you to go on to the second part of the book much surer about the rightness of your decision than you were at the start.

But it's your life, and inevitably you are the person most affected by that decision. We've asked the questions, suggested the options, offered some practical information about the ways in which you can carry out your plans to make them more realistic. But it was never intended that you'd be told what to do. No book, no advertising or media hype, no individual counsellor, friend or even your closest partner, can do that.

Decisions *are* difficult. Think of some of the important and less important ones you've made in the past. Have you never made a mistake? Have you made a decision that later seemed to be the wrong one, but later still turned out to have been correct? That's most people's experience. So you may have made a mistake now, in deciding to go ahead, or not, with the attempt to become pregnant. Or, as discussed in chapter 11, you may have been frustrated in your decision.

So yes – maybe you've made the wrong decision. Perhaps in later years you'll believe this. Or you may be doubtful about it – how can a childless person ever be absolutely sure that she isn't missing something far more rewarding than the life she's chosen for herself, or the mother of a family be sure that freedom and independence wouldn't have suited her better?

Human life occurs only once, and the reason we cannot determine which of our decisions are good and which bad is that in a given situation we can make only one decision; we are not granted a second, third or fourth life in which to compare various decisions. (Milan Kundera: *The Unbearable Lightness of Being*, 1984, Faber and Faber)

So you'll never really know. What is sure is that, in this life, there are many decisions that can't be changed, and that spending time and emotional energy on raking over the past is a recipe for depression. Whether or not you believe that you've had the decision thrust upon you (you accepted passively that you 'ought' to have a baby, or acceded to the wishes of a partner who didn't like children) or because you made that decision without any kind of outside pressure and with your eyes wide open – *it's made*.

It may seem like defeat to say to yourself that you've got to make the best of it. But what's the alternative? And there *is* a 'best'. Right through this book we've looked at all the advantages and all the disadvantages of deciding either way. So whichever way you've chosen, there are compensations, positive rewards even. Grasp them, enjoy them and build your life around them.

APPENDIX

MATERNITY BENEFITS

Since April 1987 there has been a radical change in the arrangements for maternity benefits – who is entitled to them, how they are paid, and how to claim them. The new scheme has overturned the old system and has resulted in a situation where some women who would formerly have been entitled to certain payments are not now eligible.

Maternity payment

Mothers no longer get an automatic £25 maternity grant. Only those mothers claiming Supplementary Benefit or Family Income Supplement can claim the new maternity payment. At the time of writing this payment is £75, but this could change. The DHSS office handling existing benefits provides information on claiming this payment.

You or your family will be eligible for Family Income Supplement if you're a single parent working at least 24 hours a week, or if you are a couple one of whom is working at least 30 hours a week, and your family's gross income is below a certain level. The Maternity Alliance provides the following examples:

- a family with one child under 11 with gross income below £100.70 a week
- a family with two children under 11 with gross income below £112.60
- a family with three children under 11 with gross income below £123.50.

If you have older children, or you later have another child, the income level at which you can claim FIS will be higher. You should be able to claim the new grant from 11 weeks before the birth up to 13 weeks after it, unless it is only the birth of the baby that entitles you to FIS, when you will have to claim within 13 weeks after the birth.

Maternity allowance and maternity pay

Statutory Maternity Pay has now replaced the old maternity allowance and maternity pay for some working mothers. Only those women who are self-employed or who change jobs early in their pregnancy can claim a state allowance. Some women who don't qualify for either Statutory Maternity Pay or the State Maternity Allowance, but who have previously paid National Insurance contributions, will be able to get nine weeks' sickness benefit around the time of their baby's birth – this will depend on how recently they've been in paid work and how long they have been in the same job.

Statutory Maternity Pay

This is payable by your employer when you stop work to have a baby if:

- you have worked continuously for your employer for at least 26 weeks by the fifteenth week before the expected date of confinement, and you work at least one day of the fifteenth week;
- for the last eight weeks your earnings have been enough for you to pay National Insurance contributions;
- you are still pregnant in the eleventh week before the expected week of confinement.

SMP is payable for up to 18 weeks. You can get it at 11 weeks before the expected week of confinement, or, if you prefer, you can work for longer before the baby is born and claim later. But if you work later than the seventh week before the birth you will lose some SMP. The SMP stops after 18 weeks or the eleventh week after the birth, whichever is earlier. If you start work with a different employer after the birth, it will stop earlier.

There are two rates of SMP. The higher rate applies if you have been with your employer for at least two years full-time (16 or more hours a week) or five years part-time (8–16 hours a week) by the fifteenth week before the expected week of confinement. The first six weeks' pay is fixed at nine-tenths of your normal pay. For the remaining weeks you get £32.85 a week (1987 figures). Those not eligible (see above) will get £32.85 for each week of SMP.

To claim SMP
You must write to your employer at least 21 days before you intend to leave, stating that you will be stopping work and wish to claim SMP. You must send your employer form MAT B1 (the certificate provided by doctor or midwife when you are 28 weeks pregnant) not later than the end of the third week in which you claim SMP. If you don't write to your employer or send in the MAT B1 form, you could lose your right to SMP.

There are some circumstances in which you are not entitled to SMP. These are:

• giving up work before the fifteenth week before the expected date of the birth;
• not having been with your employer for 26 weeks by that time;
• if your earnings are below the level for National Insurance contributions;
• if you didn't give your employer proof of pregnancy on form MAT B1.

If you aren't entitled to SMP your employer should give you form SMP 1 which you should take to your DHSS office to see whether you can claim State Maternity Allowance.

State Maternity Allowance

This applies to those women who are self-employed or who don't qualify for SMP, but who have worked and earned enough to pay National Insurance contributions for at least 26 out of the 52 weeks ending on the fifteenth week before the birth. This allowance is paid at £30.05 per week (1987 figures) and is claimed for the same weeks as SMP (see above). If you're in work, use the form MA 1, available at the DHSS office.

Sickness Benefit

This may be payable if you are not eligible for SMP or State Maternity Benefit because you have not been working recently, but you paid (or were credited with) National Insurance contributions on earnings of at least £1775 in the previous tax year (1987 figures). You can claim sickness benefit for nine weeks, beginning six weeks before the week of expected confinement. Ask for information at the local DHSS office.

At the time of writing it is not clear how the system will affect a large number of women who may well be worse off than they would have been before April 1987. The Maternity Alliance points out that many women will receive no financial help at all to meet the costs of a new baby, and that government proposals on employment rights could limit further equal opportunities for working women. For fuller details concerning maternity benefits and an update on the current situation, contact the Maternity Alliance, 59–61 Camden High Street, London NW1 7LJ (Telephone 01 388 6337). If you require leaflets, etc. send a large sae.

THE LEGITIMACY LAWS

It was expected that the 1986–7 session of Parliament might see a revision of the laws concerning legitimacy and inheritance, abolishing not only the word 'illegitimate' in official documents but also the whole concept of illegitimacy. Until this has been enacted, it has always been possible for the name of the father of a child born to a 'single' woman to be entered on the child's birth certificate – with his consent. The surname of the child in these or any other circumstances can be the mother's or the father's.

FURTHER READING

CHAPTER 1 A QUESTION OF IMPORTANCE

Allen, Isobel, (1985), *Counselling Services for Sterilisation, Vasectomy and Termination of Pregnancy*, Policy Studies Institute, London

Chesler, Phyllis, (1981), *With Child: A Diary of Motherhood*, Berkley Books, New York

Dowrick, Stephanie and Grundberg, Sibyl (eds), (1980), *Why Children?*, The Women's Press, London

Neustatter, Angela with Newson, Gina, (1986), *Mixed Feelings: the Experience of Abortion*, Pluto Press, London

Renvoize, Jean, (1985), *Going Solo: Single Mothers by Choice*, Routledge & Kegan Paul, London and New York

CHAPTER 2 NEGATIVE FEEDBACK

Chesler, Phyllis, (1981), *With Child: A Diary of Motherhood*, Berkley Books, New York

Herbert, Martin and Sluckin, Alice, (1983), *Maternal Bonding*, Blackwell, Oxford

CHAPTER 3 A 'STABLE RELATIONSHIP'

Badinter, Elizabeth, (1981), *The Myth of Motherhood*, Souvenir Press, London

Bottomley, Anne *et al.*, (1981), *The Cohabitation Handbook*, Pluto Press, London

Dowrick, Stephanie and Grundberg, Sibyl (eds), (1980), *Why Children?*, The Women's Press, London

Golombok, S., Spencer, A. and Rutter, M., (1983), 'Children in lesbian and single-parent households', *Journal of Child Psychology and Psychiatry*, vol. 24, pp.551–72

Mansfield, Penny, (1985), *Young People and Marriage*, Scottish Marriage Council, Edinburgh

Renvoize, Jean, (1985), *Going Solo: Single Mothers by Choice*, Routledge & Kegan Paul, London and New York

Waterman, Elyce, (1985), *Father Love*, Piatkus, London

CHAPTER 4 STAYING SINGLE

Dowrick, Stephanie and Grundberg, Sibyl (eds), (1980), *Why Children?*, The Women's Press, London

Renvoize, Jean, (1985), *Going Solo: Single Mothers by Choice*, Routledge & Kegan Paul, London and New York

Shapiro, Jean, (1985), *On Your Own: A Practical Guide to Independent Living*, Pandora, London and New York ·

Terrence Higgins Trust, 'Women and Aids', free leaflet

CHAPTER 5 SHARED CARE

Boston Women's Health Collective, (1981), *Ourselves and Our Children*, Penguin, Harmondsworth

Child Poverty Action Group, *National Welfare Benefits Handbook*, London, updated frequently

Consumers' Association, (1983), *The Legal Side of Buying a House*, London

Jackson, Brian, (1984), *Fatherhood*, Allen & Unwin, London

Mothercare catalogue, produced twice a year and available from Mothercare shops

Oakley, Ann, (1986) (reprint), *From Here to Maternity*, Penguin, Harmondsworth

Employment Rights for the Expectant Mother, (free leaflet from local employment offices published by the Department of Employment)

CHAPTER 6 HEALTHY MOTHER, HEALTHY CHILD

Bampfylde, Heather, (1984), *Countdown to a Healthy Baby*, Collins, London

Boyd, Catherine and Sellers, Lea, (1982), *The British Way of Birth*, Pan, London

Carter, Margaret, (1985), *Good Housekeeping Baby Book*, Ebury Press, London

Hanssen, Maurice, (1984), *E for Additives*, Thorsons, Wellingborough

Kitzinger, Sheila, (1983), *The New Good Birth Guide*, Penguin, Harmondsworth

Phillips, Angela, (1983), *Your Body, Your Baby, Your Life*, Pandora, London

Phillips, Angela and Rakusen, Jill (eds), (1979), *Our*

Bodies, Ourselves, Penguin, Harmondsworth
Scher, Jonathan and Dix, Carol, (1984), *Will My Baby Be Normal?*, Allen Lane, Harmondsworth
Stoppard, Dr Miriam, (1986), *Pregnancy and Birth Book*, Dorling Kindersley, London
Wesson, Nicky, (1987), *Pregnancy and Childbirth*, Thorsons, Wellingborough

CHAPTER 7 PAUSE FOR THOUGHT

Many of the books listed above, or the organisations listed on pp.178–81 should help you make up your mind. See also the general listings on p.177 and pp.180–1.

CHAPTER 8 DOWN TO EARTH

Clapham NCT Working Mothers' Group, (1982), *The Working Mother's Handbook*, (available from 167 Fentiman Road, London SW8 1JY: £1.25 including p&p)
Consumers' Association, (1983), *A Patient's Guide to the National Health Service*, London
Garner, Lesley, (1982), *How to Survive as a Working Mother*, Penguin, Harmondsworth
Health Education Council, (1984), *Pregnancy Book*, (available from ante-natal clinics)
Moss, Peter, (1980), *Nurseries Now*, Penguin, Harmondsworth
Rodwell, Lee, (1987), *Working Through Your Pregnancy*, Thorsons, Wellingborough

CHAPTER 9 INFERTILITY, SUBFERTILITY, LOSS

BAAF, (1986), *Adopting a Child*, (available from 11 Southwark Street, London SE1: £1.25)
Borg, S. and Lasker, J., (1982), *When Pregnancy Fails: Families Coping with Miscarriage, Stillbirth and Infant Death*, Routledge & Kegan Paul, London
Pfeiffer, Naomi and Woollett, Anne, (1983), *The Experience of Infertility*, Virago, London
Richardson, Diane, (1987), *Women and the AIDS Crisis*, Pandora, London
Stanway, Andrew, (1986), *Infertility: A Commonsense Guide for the Childless*, Thorsons, Wellingborough
Terrence Higgins Trust, 'Women and Aids', free leaflet
Warnock, Mary (Chairman), (1984), Warnock Report,

Command 9314, HMSO, London

Winston, Robert M.L., (1986), *Infertility: a Sympathetic Approach*, Martin Dunitz, London

Stepchildren

Inglis, Ruth, (1986), *The Good Step-Parents Guide*, Grafton Books, London

Maddox, Brenda, (1975), *Step-Parenting*, Unwin Paperbacks, London

CHAPTER 10 ANOTHER CHILD?

Bayard, Robert T. and Bayard, Jean, (1984), *Help! I've got a teenager!*, Exley, Watford

Boston Women's Health Collective, (1981), *Ourselves and Our Children*, Penguin, Harmondsworth

Douglas, Jo and Richman, Naomi, (1984), *Coping with Young Children*, Penguin, Harmondsworth

See also *Stepchildren*, above

CHAPTER 11 CHILDLESS BY CHOICE

British Organisation of Non-Parents (BON) issue three leaflets:

You Do Have a Choice, Am I Parent Material? and *No Regrets*, (available from BM Box 5866, London WC1N 3XX: send sae when making enquiries)

Pauncefort, Zandria, (1984), *Choices in Contraception*, Pan, London (includes chapters on female and male sterilisation)

Richardson, Diane, (1987), *Women and the Aids Crisis*, Pandora, London

Shapiro, Rose, (1987), *Contraception: A Practical and Political Guide*, Virago, London

CHAPTER 12 BACK TO YOU

See general list of books below and general list of organisations on pp.180–1.

GENERAL

Kitzinger, Sheila, (1985), *Woman's Experience of Sex*, Dorling Kindersley, London

Phillips, Angela, (1983), *Your Body, Your Baby, Your Life*, Pandora, London

Stoppard, Dr Miriam, (1986), *Pregnancy and Birth Book*, Dorling, Kindersley, London

The Terrence Higgins Trust, 'Women and Aids', free leaflet

LIST OF
ORGANISATIONS

CHAPTER 1 A QUESTION OF IMPORTANCE

British Organisation of Non-Parents (BON), BM Box 5866, London WC1N 3XX

CHAPTER 2 NEGATIVE FEEDBACK

The National Childbirth Trust, 9 Queensborough Terrace, London W2

CHAPTER 3 A 'STABLE RELATIONSHIP'

Brixton Black Women's Centre, 41a Stockwell Green, London SW9 (can provide information about black women's groups in the London area)

Lesbian Line, BM Box 1514; Telephone: 01 251 6911 (can provide advice and information and also telephone numbers of local sources)

London Friend, 247 Upper Street, London N1 2UA; Telephone: 01 359 7371 (help and advice for lesbian mothers)

The Meet-a-Mum Association, 26a Cumnor Hill, Oxford OX2 9HA

The National Marriage Guidance Council, Herbert Gray College, Little Church Street, Rugby

A Woman's Place, Hungerford House, Victoria Embankment, London WC2 (can provide information about women's groups)

The Women's Therapy Centre, 6 Manor Gardens, London N7

CHAPTER 4 STAYING SINGLE

British Pregnancy Advisory Service, Austry Manor, Wooten Wowen, Solihull B95 6BX; Telephone: 05642 3225 (and branches)

Gingerbread, 35 Wellington Street, London WC2E 7BN

National Council for One-Parent Families, 255 Kentish Town Road, London NW5 2LX

Rights of Women and Women's Reproductive Rights Information Centre, 52-54 Featherstone Street, London EC1Y 8RT; Telephone: 01 251 6577 (Tuesday and Thursday 7–9 p.m.)

Scottish Council for Single Parents, 13 Grayfield Square, Edinburgh EH1 3NX and 39 Hope Street, Glasgow G2 6AE

CHAPTER 6 HEALTHY MOTHER, HEALTHY CHILD

Association for Improvements in Maternity Services (AIMS), 163 Liverpool Road, London N1 0RF

Healthline; Telephone: 01 980 4848 (tape 7: drugs)

Liberation Network of People with Disabilities, 68 Alden House, Duncan Road, London E8

Maternity Alliance, 59 Camden High Street, London NW1

National Childbirth Trust, 9 Queensborough Terrace, London W2

Society to Support Home Confinements, 17 Laburnam Avenue, London SE26 (and see Further Reading and List of Organisations, general listings, p.174 and 177)

The Terrence Higgins Trust, BM AIDS, London WC1N 3XX

CHAPTER 7 PAUSE FOR THOUGHT

Many of the books listed on pp.174–7 or the organisations listed above should help you make up your mind. See also the general listings on p.177 and pp.180–1.

CHAPTER 8 DOWN TO EARTH

Association for Improvements in Maternity Services (AIMS), 163 Liverpool Road, London N1 0RF

Association of Radical Midwives, 88 The Drive, London SW20

Baxter's Agency, PO Box 12, Peterborough PE3 6JN

Consultus, 17 London Road, Tonbridge, Kent

Country Cousins, 6 Springfield Road, Horsham, West Sussex RH12 2PR (for help in emergency – 'proxy' mothers, etc)

The Job Sharing Project, 437a Upper Street, London N1 0PD

Nanny Share Register, 42 Park Road, East Molesey, Surrey

National Childcare Campaign, c/o Surrey Docks Childcare Project, Docklands Settlement, London SE16

National Childminders' Association, 13 London Road, Bromley, Kent BR1 1DE

National Nursery Examination Board, Argyle House, Euston Road, London NW1

The *Lady* magazine also carries advertisements for nannies

CHAPTER 9 INFERTILITY, SUBFERTILITY, LOSS

AIDS Helpline; Telephone: 01 278 8745 (7–10 p.m.)

The Foundation for the Study of Infant Deaths, 5th Floor, 4 Grosvenor Place, London SW1

The Miscarriage Association, 4 Ashfield Terrace, Thorpe, Wakefield, West Yorkshire

National Association for the Childless, 318 Summer Lane, Birmingham B19 3RL

Stillbirth and Neonatal Death Society, 37 Christchurch Hill, London NW3 1LA

The Terrence Higgins Trust, BM AIDS, London WC1N 3XX

Women's Reproductive Rights Information Centre, 52–54 Featherstone Street, London EC1Y 8RT (for contacts with infertility groups)

Stepchildren

National Stepfamily Association, Ross Street Community Centre, Ross Street, Cambridge CB1 3BS; Telephone counselling: 0223 460313 (Sunday and Friday 7–10 p.m., Monday and Wednesday 2–5 p.m.)

CHAPTER 11 CHILDLESS BY CHOICE

British Organisation of Non-Parents (BON), BM Box 5866, London WC1N 3XX

GENERAL

British Pregnancy Advisory Service, Austry Manor, Wooten Wowen, Solihull B95 6BX; Telephone 05642 3225 (and branches)

Child Poverty Action Group, 1 Macklin Street, London WC2B 5NH, and 132 Lauriston Place, Edinburgh

Family Network; Telephone: 01 226 2033 ('phone-in service for parents under stress)

Foundation for Women's Health Research and Development, Africa Centre, 38 King Street, London WC2E 8JT

Healthline; Telephone: 01 980 4848 for tape-recorded advice on health topics. The line is open from 2–10 p.m. daily. Topics include: 121 nutrition in pregnancy; 124 post-natal depression; 68 sterilisation; 128 unplanned pregnancy and agencies for help; 136 AIDS; ask the operator for other topics (eg drugs) and they will be played to you if available

The Maternity Alliance, 59 Camden High Street, London NW1

The Patients' Association, Room 33, 18 Charing Cross Road, London WC2

Women's Health Information Centre, 52–54 Featherstone Street, London EC1Y 8RT; Telephone: 01 251 6580

Women's Reproductive Rights Information Centre, 52–54 Featherstone Street, London EC1Y 8RT; Telephone: 01 251 6332

INDEX

PANDORA HANDBOOKS

Our selection of handbooks designed to represent the changing lives of women today is growing fast:

ON YOUR OWN
A Practical Guide to Independent Living
by Jean Shapiro
A bible for all women learning for the first time to live on their own, the book covers all the practical and emotional matters that women are likely to face in these circumstances, from organising holidays and managing money to keeping fit and well and managing the menopause.
0–86358–045–9 illustrated paperback

BIRTH AND OUR BODIES
Exercises and Meditations for the Childbearing Year and Preparation for an Active Birth
by Paddy O'Brien
Working from pre-conception to the birth, this practical and positive companion guide provides women with detailed physical and mental exercises to practise through pregnancy and childbirth.
0–86358–047–5 illustrated paperback

YOUR BODY, YOUR BABY, YOUR LIFE
by Angela Phillips with Nicky Lean and Barbara Jacobs
Written by the UK co-editor of *Our Bodies, Ourselves*, a non-patronising, non-moralising, non-sexist guide to pregnancy and childbirth. Widely praised and now a classic.
0–86358–006–8 illustrated paperback

RUNNING
The Women's Handbook
by Liz Sloan and Ann Kramer
With illustrations by Jo Nesbitt and Elaine Anderson
A handbook for the thousands of women who run or
want to start running – enabling women to lead a
fitter, freer life.
0–86358–043–2 illustrated paperback

NATURAL HEALING IN GYNECOLOGY
A Manual for Women
by Rina Nissim
'Provides a wealth of healing alternatives from eastern
and western cultures and critiques the limits of
conventional western medicine giving us the power
of choice. Its friendly conversational style is a delight,
as though a wise woman were guiding us through
whatever problem we have and helping us figure out
what to do. An unusual and invaluable resource
indeed.' – Boston Women's Health Collective
0–86358–069–6 illustrated paperback

FIT FOR THE FUTURE
The Guide for Women Who Want to Live Well
by Jeanette Winterson
A complete manual for any woman who wants to live
well, providing a philosophy of fitness which is
compulsive – covers exercise, diet, sex, sports. . . .
0–86358–053–X illustrated paperback

WOMEN AND THE AIDS CRISIS
by Diane Richardson
'The first well-documented book on women and
AIDS to appear in a form accessible to the non-
professional public. . . . It is original, thought-
provoking and timely. Any reader who does not
emerge with a warmer compassion and understanding
of the problems must be a harsh individual indeed.' –
Janet Green (Counselling Administrator, Terrence
Higgins Trust)
0–86358–189–7 paperback

For further information about Pandora Press publications contact: 11 New Fetter Lane, London EC4P 4EE, England or Methuen Inc., 29 West 35th Street, New York, NY 10001, USA.